The AMY BINEGAR-KIMMES-LYLE

BOOK OF FAILURES

D0770034

A funny memoir by

Amy Lyle

Many stories in this book are true.

But some are lies.

GERMAN PROVERB

As my husband[1] and I planned our wedding, my grandparents were celebrating sixty years of marriage. My grandmother, a woman of few words, offered me esteemed advice: "Let it be known. There will be very good decades and very bad decades." And there were.

---

[1] First husband.

A LITTLE BIT ABOUT ME

I've been married twenty years, not to the same people, but twenty years nonetheless. I understand that a successful marriage requires being a good listener, showing sensitivity toward others' needs and wants, and practicing unconditional love. I really struggle with being a good listener, showing sensitivity toward others' needs and wants, and unconditional love. I do, however, offer loyalty and humor and I am a real wildcat in the bedroom.[2]

Everyone tells you to marry your best friend but I take exception to this advice and have the divorce papers to prove it. Your best friend knows who's on the list of people you wish you could stab in the face; knows all your aches and ailments; is the one that helps you try to narrow down whether you have diverticulitis, irritable bowel syndrome, or a tumor in your digestive tract—things you tell your best friend, not the person you're having sex with.

Before we got married, my second husband, Peter, asked me if I was certain I could handle four children.[3] "Sure!" I answered confidently. I was a corporate trainer for one of the biggest staffing firms in the world and thought, *They're just kids. How difficult could it be?* In hindsight, I gravely miscalculated the

---

[2] I'm not a wildcat in the bedroom.
[3] When Peter and I got married, his daughters were 10 and 12, his son was eight and my daughter, 6.

prospect. I imagine it's like Katie Holmes agreeing to marry Tom Cruise. She presumably thought, *So he believes in a Galactic Confederacy where people arrived on a DC-8-like spacecraft seventy-five million years ago ... he's adorable!*

Sometimes you just get swept away in the moment and think you can handle anything. It was only AFTER Peter and I got married that I realized that four kids are way too many kids.

I knew I could succumb to defeat or keep trying. I opted for the latter and now live by the motto: I am not a failure. ... I'm just having a little bit of trouble right now.

BLENDING FAMILIES CAN BE ... PROBLEMATIC

Peter's Approach:
Peter to kids: You lied about picking up your room. You have broken trust. I think it was Luke—let me look it up (looks up verse on phone)—yes, Luke 16:10. "Whoever can be trusted with very little can also be trusted with much, and whoever is dishonest with very little will also be dishonest with much." Do you understand what that means? If I can't trust you to make your bed, how can I trust you to drive a car? Or go on a date? I lied to my dad once and our relationship was never the same. We are all citizens in this house and you have a very small, yet extremely critical role in this household. One day, you will have your own house. Hey! Did you roll your eyes? That is disrespectful!

Kids: You—
Peter: Do not interrupt me. Let's discuss why I must tell you a thousand times. When I was a boy—
Kids: Oh my gosh.
Peter: Are you interrupting me again? I'm taking your phone for the day.
Kids: What?
Peter: Oh really? Now it's two days ...

My Approach:
Me to kids: Hey, where are you going?

Kids: Out.

Me: You didn't clean your room so you're not going out.

Kids: What?

Me: Clean your room or you'll be in tomorrow night too. I'm going to the movies. See you later.

Peter and I may not agree on the process of discipline but we have common ground on a consequence that works—manual labor.

Issue	Consequence
Sassy	Scrub the baseboards
Fighting with siblings	Wash the windows
Bad language	Mop the floors
Lying	Scrub shower grout
Late for curfew	Detail the cars

Our neighbors ask us, "Why do your kids always smell like Windex and Lysol?"

I'M A RIVER RAT

I grew up in Marietta, Ohio, which is in the thick of the Appalachian region. It has been suggested that it's an area filled with people that are partial to moonshine and prone to acts of violence. I don't disagree. However, I believe if you go fifty miles outside any major city, you'll find a similar crowd.

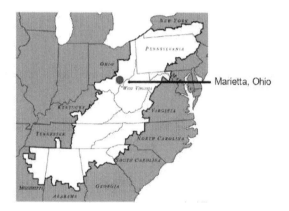

Marietta, Ohio

Marietta is a beautiful town known for its haunted hotel, The Lafayette, outstanding antique shops and the headquarters of *Bird Watcher ' s Digest*.

Growing up in Marietta, crime was never an issue. We slept with our doors unlocked. There's only one murder about every thirty years and most of the crimes listed in the paper deal with stolen mail and people shooting deer within city limits.

Marietta has two large hospital systems, several manufacturing plants and a small liberal arts college. It's a great place to raise a family.

Oddly, when I searched Marietta's crime data online, NeighborhoodScout.com ranked it in the *lowest* 90 percent of safest cities in the United States,[4] placing Marietta's safety between Compton and Detroit.

I'm here to tell you, that's a damn lie.

CRIME INDEX

9

(100 is safest)

Safer than 9% of U.S. Cities

---

[4] www.neighborhoodscout.com/oh/marietta/crime11

WHERE IN THE WORLD?

In the early 1980s, if you needed to research a project for school, you went to the library to check out books or use the microfiche machine which was needed to read microcards. Documents such as old newspapers were imaged onto small cards that looked like negatives from an old camera. The microfilm card was placed into a microfiche reader to display the data. You couldn't make a copy of the information on our machine; you could only LOOK at the data and take notes, in a notebook, with a pencil.

Microfiche reader

My assignment was to research a country in Africa. I've never mastered the Dewey decimal book classification system that's required to locate actual books in a library, so I stuck to microfilm and the *Encyclopedia Britannica*.

I picked Rhodesia so I could share my outrage regarding how the British were presiding over their property, metals, and resources and how the Shona tribe had been unsuccessful in their revolts.

Preparing to present to my class, I set up a huge map that I had drawn using two poster boards, markers and Elmer's glue (to add texture to the topography).

The morning of my presentation, I passionately spoke of how the Rhodesians had been trapped for so long under the thumb of the British and how the United States should step in to help them gain independence. I implored my fellow students to write their senators, Howard Metzenbaum, George Voinovich and John Glenn, as I had done, asking for an end to the oppression of the Rhodesians.

My social studies teacher asked me to stay after class. I thought for sure she was going to nominate me to represent our school in some sort of state or maybe even national social studies capacity. Instead, she shared that Rhodesia *had* gained their independence from England in *1970* and was officially renamed Zimbabwe in 1980.

Africa before 1965

Africa after 1965

My local library was built in the early 1900s with Andrew Carnegie funds and was behind on updating material. The map and encyclopedias I had used were over twenty years old. I had missed the news of the brutal civil war and eventual official independence, as well as the changing of the name "Rhodesia" to "Zimbabwe" by a few significant years. Even with my Elmer's glue added for topography texture, she gave me a D.

Senators Metzenbaum, Voinovich and Glenn never replied to my "Free Rhodesia" requests.

SAY AGAIN?

From my parents, I inherited a love of reading. A few years ago, I set a goal to read more of the classics, and since then I've read many of the works of Plath, Faulkner, Hemingway, Charlotte Bronte and Salinger. I loved Steinbeck's *East of Eden*, Tolstoy's *Anna Karenina* and *War and Peace*, Fitzgerald's *Gatsby* and every book by or about Jane Austen. I made it through Melville and Dickens but would not recommend them. I also read contemporary fiction: Toni Morrison, Wally Lamb, Jennifer Weiner and Rick Bragg are a few of my go-to, current-day authors. I'm obsessed with comedy books. My favorites are by Jenny Lawson, *Let's Pretend This Never Happened* and *Furiously Happy;* as well as works by comedian/authors Tina Fey, Amy Poehler, Carol Burnett, Judd Apatow, David Sedaris, Ellen DeGeneres, Roseanne Barr, Jim Gaffigan, Rachel Dratch, Aisha Tyler and Jerry Seinfeld.

Being such a voracious reader, it doesn't make sense that I cannot pronounce anything. Researching this issue, I found possible causes in an article entitled "Common Speech and Language Disorders." I cannot pronounce my disorders which are aphasia and dysarthria, but here are the causes:

Aphasia	Dysarthria
Alzheimer's disease	Alcohol intoxication

Brain tumor	Diseases such as cerebral palsy, myasthenia gravis, or multiple sclerosis (MS)
Dementia	Dementia
Stroke	Facial trauma
Transient ischemic attack (TIA)	Head and neck cancer surgery
Head trauma	Head trauma
	Neurological disorders such as Parkinson's disease or Huntington's disease
	Poorly fitting dentures

I do suffer occasionally from the dysarthria explanation of "alcohol intoxication," but I have just as many issues when I'm sober, which makes me sound permanently mentally impaired, not drunk. My SAT scores would prove that I'm completely average.

Currently, I'm reading a remarkable book by Vikram Seth titled *A Suitable Boy*. I'm only halfway through and already have a list of words I can't pronounce:

colloquy, grandiloquent, irascible, avuncularity, cyclostyled, ignominy, obsequiousness, puerility, licentious, myocardial, cognoscenti, ameliorative, perennially, querulous, labyrinthine,

13

imbued, wastrels, thumri, perspicacity, censorious, bharatanatyam, angarkha, vociferously, invigilator, jodhpurs, insouciance, superciliously, promulgated, desiccated, pincered and obstreperous, bumptious, blancmange, voluble, ecumenical and pabulum.

I emailed my friend Kristin, who is a speech pathologist, asking why I can't pronounce anything. She immediately replied:

 Kristin Upite
to me ▾

1) **Being Appalachian**
2) Articulation Disorder (can't pronounce certain sounds/substitutes some sounds for others)
3) Anomia (can't remember the names of things/objects)
4) Apraxia (problems coordinating muscles to make sounds)

You can take the girl out of Appalachia ... you know how it goes.

SIDE EFFECTS

The day my first husband, Mr. Kimmes, and I decided to get divorced was a Sunday. I remember because I looked forward to the HBO lineup of *The Wire*, *Sex and the City* and *The Sopranos* on Sundays. We were putting clean sheets on our bed when he said casually, "I think we should separate." After five years of dating, eight years of marriage, one daughter, two cats, two dogs, one failed business and sheer exhaustion, just like that, it was over.

We had stayed together so long after not wanting to be together that neither one of us had any fight left in us. It took all of a minute to split up what we had accumulated in thirteen years. "You take the Bernhardt furniture; I'll take the Ethan Allen." I got the china and nice silverware; he got the riding lawnmower and wine collection. The only thing left was the formality of standing in front of a judge and admitting that when we agreed to the "until death do us part" part, we had lied.

My lawyer's paralegal called and asked me to come in to "look over some papers." I booked the appointment for one o'clock, right after my OB-GYN appointment because the offices were less than a mile apart.

While I was on the examining table in the OB-GYN's office, my doctor said, "You seem really stressed." I'm not sure how she picked up on that by examining my cervix, but I guess going through a divorce, moving out of my house, going back to work full-time and having my daughter only part-time was taking its toll, even on my insides.

"I'm getting divorced," I said.

"Well, if you're planning on having another child, you had better hurry up. You're already almost forty." Crying while a speculum is inside you is never a good idea; the more I whimpered, the more pressure I could feel. The second she exited my cervix, she gave me a sample pack of Xanax.

"I don't do well with any medication," I told her.

"You have a lot of anxiety. This will help you."

I read the back of the Xanax box: *affects chemicals in the brain that may be unbalanced in people with anxiety.* I was unbalanced. I took one tiny pill, paid the copay and was off to the lawyer's office.[5]

Waiting on my lawyer, I helped myself to a few of their magazines. I don't feel that taking magazines from lawyers' offices is stealing because they have multiple copies of each publication and they charge $240 an hour for their lawyering. Anyway, as I was trying to pretend like I was straightening my purse to hide confiscated copes of *Architectural Digest*, I heard my name.

It's so embarrassing when they call your name at a divorce attorney's office: everybody knows you have made a monumental mistake. Their looks range from "you poor dear" to "you probably deserved it."

The paralegal sat down next to me and flipped through a set of papers: "Sign here, here, initial here, sign here and ... you're

---

[5] I also put my pants back on.

divorced." She could tell I was shocked—she'd previously told me nothing would be final until we sat in front of a judge. "Everything was so amicable, the judge signed it. Congratulations. You're a divorcee."

That word *divorcee* is one of the reasons women wait so long to get divorced. No woman has ever gotten divorced and then posted on her timeline "I'm a divorcee!" It is one of worst words in the English language, rivaling "smear" and "phlegm."

I knew I was paying a divorce attorney to get divorced, but having an appointment to "look over some paperwork" and then suddenly finding myself officially divorced after thirteen years … well, I was caught off guard.

The paralegal handed me a tissue and led me by the elbow out to the elevator to the parking garage. My mind started racing. What impact would the divorce have on my daughter? How could I afford to buy another house unless I was promoted? Would I ever have sex again?

About halfway home I started to feel like there was a refrigerator on my chest. I tried to inhale deeply, but couldn't. I broke out in a cold sweat. I called Sharon, my best friend and crisis manager, and ranted between strained breaths about my cervical exam, taking the Xanax, getting three new copies of *Architectural Digest* and the news of already being divorced. Sharon talked to me until I pulled into her driveway.

When she opened my car door, I collapsed. She called 911, explaining that I "had collapsed, had severe chest pain and shortness of breath." They were on their way.

When the EMTs arrived, I was in the fetal position with Sharon spooning me in her bed. The EMTs quizzed Sharon: "Has she had any previous health or heart issues? Has this happened before? Is she a drug user?"

Sharon, always the defender of my morality and dignity, said, "For God's sake, no. She just found out she's divorced and her doctor gave her a Xanax."

Both EMTs' shoulders dropped, disappointed I wasn't a more serious case requiring BVM ventilations, oxygen or at least the insertion of an oropharyngeal airway. "Anxiety attack," they said in nonchalant unison.

"She took a Xanax FOR anxiety," Sharon reminded them.

"It's called a paradoxical reaction, when the effect of the drug is opposite to the effect expected, like pain medication causing pain. Don't let her take any more of those. Just try to get her to relax."

Within half an hour, Sharon and I were watching Tyler Perry's *Big Mamma's House 2*, eating ice cream on the sofa and ordering Chinese dumplings from our favorite delivery place, Asian Table.

Do not schedule a pap smear the same morning as your appointment with your divorce attorney—it's too much probing for one day.

CALL FROM SHARON
THE VAGINA CALL

Sharon and I have been friends for fifteen years and are at equal levels of crazy-town. She's very busy running a painting company but calls me daily with ridiculous plots and schemes, injustices and fascinating facts. When I answer her call, it's always as if I have missed the first few minutes of the conversation. I have peppered in a few of her calls throughout the book.

Me: Hello?

Sharon: My vagina's too clean.

Me: What?

Sharon: I'm at the gynecologist's office … (incoherent chatter …)

Me: What's going on? Unusual cells? STD?

Sharon: NO! There was a guy in the elevator and I couldn't talk. The doctor said my vagina's too clean and that's why I'm having issues.

Me: Hmm … I would think a vajayjay could never be to clean.

Sharon: (Incoherent mumbling ending with …) Merry Christmas.

Me: What?

Sharon: I just saw the lady that works at the Publix Deli, Martha. You know Martha—she's the one that turned me on to the store-brand turkey. It's just as good—or better—than the pricey brands. It's changed my life. She's getting one of her moles checked on the fourth floor.

Me: Oh.

Sharon: She said not to put any soap on it.

Me: On what?

Sharon: Your Vagina! She said to let your body clean itself, otherwise you are creating a hostile environment. Don't even ... wait a second.

Sharon to Wendy's drive-thru guy: Can I get a number two with cheese, no onion, ice tea—not sweet!

Sharon to me: Don't even use the shower sprayer. That's like douching ... Wait.

Sharon to Wendy's guy: No! Not sweet, unsweet! Yes, ice, of course, geez!

Sharon to me: And if you ever take a bath, you are just sitting in your own filth. Do you hear me? Stop taking baths, you're in your filth. I gotta get my burger. Bye.

GETTING DIVORCED SUCKS

After the divorce, on the ex's weekends with our daughter, I would crawl into bed Friday night and not come out until Sunday morning—aside from getting a granola bar, taking a potty break or crying in the bathtub.

Six months in, I threw myself into work and devoured Christian self-help books that include *Bounce Back: When Your Heart Is Empty and Your Dreams Are Lost*, by Julie Clinton, and *Should I Stay or Go: Divorce and God's Grace*, by Mary Lou Redding. The books made me feel like no one should ever get divorced. But too late, I was. I did take comfort that God could not love me any more OR any less and that He had a plan for me. I read the secular books my boss suggested, such as *Who Moved My Cheese*, by Spencer Johnson, MD, and *Men Are from Mars, Women Are from Venus*, by John Gray, which confirmed what I already knew: I hate change and I have zero understanding of the opposite sex.

I'm lucky to be surrounded by smart women who forced me to snap out of my funk. My friend, Marjorie, told me, "There are few things that a good haircut and new panties can't fix," which I have discovered works for both heartbreak and pneumonia recovery. After I hit the one-year anniversary of my divorce, my girlfriends announced that I needed to "get back out there."

Sharon's sweet husband, Scott, is like my older brother, except he's a few months younger than I am. He's wiser so he SEEMS older. Scott set me up a (blind) double date with one of his business associates, describing my date as "a nice-looking marketing guy that plays tennis and goes to church."

"Great!" I exclaimed, as I was feeling, as we say in the South, on fire for Jesus after all my Christian workbooks. We agreed to meet marketing/tennis guy at a Thai restaurant.

When we pulled into a parking spot and saw marketing/tennis guy waving wildly with a giant smile on his face, Sharon nudged Scott and said, "Good God, you set Amy up with someone who hasn't been laid in years!" Scott furiously defended his date selection on personality and character, plus marketing/tennis guy had already seen us, so we went in.

Marketing/tennis guy said that he hadn't played tennis lately because of a severe groin issue. Sharon kicked Scott under the table, feeling vindicated in her "Hasn't been laid in ten years" comment.

When marketing/tennis guy told us, "The last time I gave a urine sample, it had an olive in it," followed by "I have good-looking kids—thank goodness my wife cheats on me," the table got quiet. Sharon, Scott and I all sipped our drinks and waited. "I DON'T GET NO RESPECT," he screamed. "Rodney Dangerfield!" Just then, the waitstaff came over. "RODNEY DANGERFIELD," he told them, "I DON'T GET NO RESPECT." The staff asked if he needed to see the manager.

Over green-tea ice cream, he listed all the Jewish comics that he loved and could relate to because he was Jewish. He started imitating several comics, including Billy Crystal, Adam Sandler, Jerry Seinfeld, Larry David and Woody Allen, reminding us that they "are geniuses, all of them, and they all are Jewish!" Sharon, Scott and I agreed that yes, THEY were all geniuses.

After a very long period of silence, marketing/no tennis guy pretended to get an important work call, even though it was Saturday, and his phone didn't ring. I never heard from him again. How's that for no respect?

I WAS NOT TALKING TO YOU

In 2008, when I was between husbands, I noticed a very attractive man trying to get my attention in the lane next to me. By "trying to get my attention," I mean he was waving, honking and pointing like he wanted me to pull over.

Normally I would avoid a man waving and pointing at me to pull over, but females outnumber males in Atlanta by almost 100,000, so I chose to risk it.

I tried not to look directly at him as I wanted him to think I was above getting hit on in a moving car, barreling down Abernathy Road in Atlanta at lunchtime. I sped up and switched lanes and was surprised to see that he followed. Approaching a red light, I checked my mirror, slapped on some colored lip gloss, popped a mint into my mouth, and tried to act casual, as he pulled next to me and stopped.

He honked and motioned for me to roll down my window. "Hey," he said, "I was trying to get your attention for a while."

"Oh really?" I said, tossing my hair a little for dramatic effect. I could see that his car was very tidy, a very underrated trait in a man, and he was wearing a nice suit with a polka-dot tie, which to me says, *I'm serious, but yet I can be playful.* As I was fantasizing about where we would vacation together, he yelled, "The belt of your coat has been dragging down Abernathy for miles."

"Ohhhhhhhh, thanks," I countered, hopeful he would continue what was already a mini-relationship in my mind. Pulling someone over to tell her that her belt was dragging was very considerate on many levels. He was concerned about my safety and that I might be ruining my garment.

I must have been staring off into space as I wondered if his parents had a vacation home in the mountains and would let us use it when I was jolted back to reality. The car behind me was honking at me. The light had turned green, and he had already sped off, without even a wave goodbye.

I CAN SEE YOUR BUTTONS

Being single forced me to go places I never wanted to go, like the gym. I would drag myself there and watch reruns of *Sex and the City* as I walked on the treadmill two miles per hour enjoying 2,000-calorie chocolate protein smoothies. I gained five pounds.

I tried Zumba and "Power Bar Class" but I am a threat to myself and others, as I have two left feet and zero balance. As I was enjoying my third episode of *Sex and the City*, one man after another seemed to be going out of his way to pause in front of my treadmill, give me a nod or smile, then move along. The attention was surprising, but it was summer and I had a little bit of a tan, so I was feeling more confident than normal in my white wife-beater tank and designer—yet slightly irregular—yoga pants from TJ Maxx.

I jacked up the treadmill to 3 mph and sucked in my stomach. Another man walked by and smiled. I thought to myself, *my mother must be right—I'm gaining muscle.* I felt so good I started a slow jog. After two minutes of jogging I was completely winded, dripping in sweat, a little dizzy and very thirsty.

As I headed to the ladies' room I caught a glimpse of myself in the huge wall mirror. All I could see was an enormous nipple smashed up against a sweaty white T-shirt—oh my gosh, it was my own nipple! My sports bra had curled up under my left boob, elevating it several inches above the other. I looked like a lopsided participant in a wet T-shirt contest.

Telling someone that their sweaty nipple has accidentally fled the confines of their sports bra falls into the same category as the "something in your teeth rule." If someone has any humanity whatsoever, they will tell you when you have a piece of broccoli in your teeth and/or when your left nipple is on the loose. What is wrong with people? I decided then and there that I would quit the gym. As I headed out, I stepped on the scale one last time.

I'd gained two pounds.

DO YOU COME HERE OFTEN?

Coincidentally, the same night I was on the worst date ever with the Rodney Dangerfield wanna-be impersonator, I met a very tall and handsome guy named Peter III. He would ask me out and I will lie and say I was busy; trying to play hard to get; when really, I was already researching him on Ancestry.com and picking out Irish names for our future children together. We ended up dating for over a year.

Unfortunately, he was a snob. If you have ever dated a snob, you know it's flattering ... at first. Snobs are very elitist and make you feel privileged that they PICKED YOU! However, when a snob who was initially charmed by witty comebacks and silly dance moves eventually sees the real you (skirt tucked into underwear, broccoli in teeth) the fascination wears off. I allowed myself to feel inferior to the Prada-clad son of one of Cincinnati's elite.

Peter III was also obsessed with golf and his job in sales allowed him to be on the links during the week with clients. Then, every Friday night there was a club event to attend and he played Saturdays and Sundays. He would choose to play golf over anything[6] in the world. Clearly, he had an addiction.

After he'd canceled with me for the fourth time because his boss or his friend "needed a fourth," I'd had enough. I wrote

---

[6] Literally, *anything*.

him a heartfelt letter about reorganizing his priorities, how playing golf seven days was ridiculous, and that he needed to choose: me or golf.

Peter III chose golf. Within the year, he moved back to Cincinnati, got married and is expecting his first baby. Good for him.[7]

---

[7] I'm still bitter about the whole thing.

A BETTER PETER

While I was dating golfing Peter III, my friend, Marjorie, wanted to set me up with her friend, Peter Lyle. The strange part of the introduction between Peter Lyle and I was that, at one time, we had lived five houses apart but didn't know one another. He lived on Woodbury Creek and I had lived on Woodbury Point. For the nine years that we lived in the same neighborhood, I had seen Peter a hundred times and he would never wave at me. Even if I walked his cul-de-sac with my cute golden retriever, he would barely give me a nod. I found him un-neighborly.

And, my sister had previously had a crush on him. Traci was divorced and working as a swimming instructor and had the three Lyle children in her class. She told me that he would come in to pick up the kids in his work clothes and not even care that they jumped all over him soaking wet. I told her I knew exactly who he was and that he was not neighborly. (Peter's only memory of me was that he thought my golden retriever must not have come from a good breeder because her head was way too pointy; well-bred retrievers have block heads.)

Anyway, fast forward to my divorce, moving out of the neighborhood, dating the too-much-golfing Peter, breaking up with him, and Marjorie saying she wanted me to "Just talk to the new Peter—Peter Lyle." She had told Peter that I was sort of a princess (high maintenance) yet I often swore like a sailor. He thought that was an interesting combination and agreed to message me on Facebook.

Marjorie had told me he was an engineer and I already knew he seemed somewhat antisocial from his whole anti-wave stance, but for two months we messaged back and forth. Finally, I messaged: "I do have a phone" and gave him my number. He called me one second later, shocking me with his southern accent. He was *"fixin'* to pick the children up from *scole 'round fo-wah."* [8]

I called Marjorie immediately and voiced my concerns about his southern drawl. She tried to put me at ease: "He's from Atlanta. What did you expect? Just go on an actual date with him."

Peter cooked for me on our first date, making the most delicious scallops and a fancy wilted spinach dish. We danced in my kitchen and he picked me up and set me on the kitchen counter to kiss me. Within months we were married. My sister held a grudge for years.

---

[8] Translation: he was going to pick the children up from school around four.

OPPOSITES ATTRACT?

Peter is from Georgia; I'm from Ohio. He is very proud of his southern heritage; I blame my roots for most of my shortcomings. I happen to know he's embarrassed that I'm from the north because he introduces me as coming from "southern Ohio," as if that will lessen the blow. Southerners aren't partial to Ohio, as it was the birthplace of Civil War General William T. Sherman. Apparently, every self-respecting southerner was taught to despise him from listening to *Gone with the Wind,* while in utero.

In addition to our north/south differences, Peter is left-brained, and I am right-brained. As an engineer, he enjoys making and following rules. I have always gotten away with bending the rules because as a sales person, if your numbers are good, you are granted a lot of flexibility and forgiveness. Peter is very anal about details. It rattles him that I never know how much money is in my checkbook and I don't put events on our "Family Calendar." I think he's too rigid, always talking about paying the mortgage, health insurance and saving for the kids' college.

As a health consultant, he has to put together very complex acquisitions for hospitals that require years of preparation and negotiations. He approaches complex business challenges and loading the dishwasher with the same methodical precision. It can create a lot of tension in our house when everything is so important.

One night, a project that he had been working on got sideways and at 7 p.m. on a Tuesday, he was on the phone trying to push the project along while also preparing for the Boy Scouts' "Crossing the Bridge Ceremony" that was starting in half an hour.

Pacing, Peter said into the phone, "By Friday, you have to have the APA including the FMV and then we'll decide if an EA or a PSA is more appropriate. If the metrics on the FMV are favorable, then draft the LOI."

As he hung up the phone, he started rummaging through some boxes laid out on our bed. "This acquisition holdup is costing the hospital $50,000 a day, the attorney's still missing the data from the regulators AND we may have to postpone the Crossing the Bridge Ceremony because no one can find the Webelos'[9] ceremonial neckerchiefs!"

I tried to look very concerned but he caught me resisting a smile.

"You know," he said, "when we first got married, I thought you were just trying to play everything cool, but I'm starting to believe that on many levels you truly just do not give two shits."[10]

---

[9] Webelos, pronounced "WEE-buh-lohs" is a program that prepares younger boys for Boy Scouts. The term means WE"LL BE LOYal Scouts.
[10] There are very few things about which I even give one s***, and why not try to find the humor in every situation?

SOMETIMES MORE IS MORE

On one of my first dates with Peter (the now hubby) we went to a swanky restaurant in downtown Atlanta. Toward the end of our dinner the waiter came to the table with a three-tiered dessert tray and described our after-dinner options. "We have fresh berries with mascarpone limoncello cream, mango basil vacherin, crepe cake, creme brulee, a flourless chocolate torte and a strawberry cheesecake trifle."

Peter saw my internal battle between the chocolate torte versus the berries and said, "We'll take all of them."

The waiter looked confused. "Sir?"

"The desserts, we'll take one of each."

It was at that moment that I realized he was marriage material.

KIA DOUGHNUT

After putting my three-year-old daughter through a divorce, my returning to work full-time, and moving, I thought the child at least deserved to pick out a hamster. We named her Annabelle.

Annabelle

I bought a cute little box that was lined with silk dyed dark purple. It was so adorable when Annabelle would curl up in the box to sleep, like a little toy. Annabelle and Anna loved each other so much. Anna would let her roll around in the little hamster ball, put her in her purse to go to the store and even sneak Annabelle into her bed (which resulted in 1,000 tiny poops). After having her for only a few weeks, we were sad to find Annabelle dead in her little purple box.[11] Anna wanted another Annabelle immediately. I thought we should get a more durable rodent.

I got an email saying an equine rescue group had found HUNDREDS of guinea pigs in a horse barn that were available

---

[11] Annabelle had eaten the box and I must assume the cloth dye poisoned her, or she could have died from natural causes.

for immediate adoption. We picked one out that had the markings of a black-and-white Holstein cow. Anna named her adorable guinea pig Baxter Tater Muffin. She would put Baxter Tater Muffin in a baby doll stroller and walk him around the block. All the neighbors got to know him and would stop and ask Anna, "How's Baxter Tater Muffin?"

We had been raising Baxter for three years when I married Peter, and when Peter's ten-year-old daughter, Maddy, wanted a guinea pig for her birthday, we let her pick one out from the pet store. She named her pig Trixie Krystal. Baxter Tater Muffin and Trixie Krystal immediately got married and started a family. Within what seemed like weeks, the baby guinea pigs started families and within months we had fourteen guinea pigs. I started to give them as presents to any kid that was going to a birthday party and put ads on our neighborhood Internet site for "Free Pigs." Finally, we were down to three: the two lady pigs and one gentleman pig that we put into separate hutches.

Guinea pig Kia Doughnut was the firstborn child of Baxter Tater Muffin and Trixie Krystal. The kids brought Kia to me, saying her eyeball "looked gross." I told Peter we were taking Kia to the vet. "Her eye looks swollen and she may need some drops."

Kia with cone

Kia was returned with only one eyeball and a three-hundred-dollar vet bill.

Even with only one eyeball, Kia lived a full life, rotating between a huge timothy-hay-filled trough in our garage and an outdoor hutch in our backyard. She died peacefully in her sleep at age seven.

DON'T MAKE ME KILL YOU

Peter doesn't sleep. He likes to say he "doesn't need a lot of sleep," but the truth is he's artificially awake from caffeine. He drinks six coffee/tea/soda drinks every day.

While I'm trying to go to sleep, he reads *Garden & Gun* magazine and says, "Look at this—it's a La Cornue Grand Palais Range, forty-eight thousand dollars. Is that cobalt blue, honey? Do you think that is cobalt blue?"

"No! I want you to turn out the light!" I bark. He turns out the light but still isn't sleepy so he checks his emails and texts on his phone. "Tap, tap, tap, tap, tap," I hear as he texts. "I can hear that," I say, so he turns it down, but the glow of the phone is so bright I cover my head with pillows to try to fall asleep.

Sometimes I wake up and his foot is an inch from my face. "I have a cramp! I have a cramp! Rub the arch of my foot!" When I hear earth-shaking snoring, I know he has finally fallen asleep. That's when I start gently tapping him, but I'll escalate all the way to shaking him if needed. "What? What? Why are you waking me up?" he asks.

"You're snoring," I say.

"I don't snore," he says, and goes back to sleep.

In the morning, I try to appeal to his health by mentioning that he isn't breathing for about twenty seconds at a time throughout the night and without oxygen he could die. He says,

"I don't think so. I feel great." I record him on my phone and email him the video.

"Do you see?" I ask.

Peter says flatly, "You are so weird! You have all these demands just to be able to sleep. Who needs darkness and quiet to sleep?"

The snoring continued for six years, over 2,000 nights, which explains why I look like I do—beat down. Even with a pillow over my head and wearing headphones playing whale noises, I could still hear the snoring. One night I cracked. I shook him until he woke. I was sobbing and screaming about how depriving someone of sleep is torture.

"That's what they do during Navy Seals' training and when they need to extract secrets from prisoners of war. They deprive them of sleep!" I took my pillow and marched to the door. "You have to go to a sleep clinic or we can't sleep in the same bed."

The requirements of the sleep clinic are … sleeping. They hook you up to a bunch of wires that monitor your brain activity, eye movement, heart rate, blood-oxygen levels, snoring and airflow. They provide a report of the activity.

Peter was shocked by his results. "Oh my god! I had eighty-two events!" I'm not up on sleep-clinic vernacular and looked confused. Peter continued, "I stopped breathing eighty-two times in one night! My oxygen level is really, really low. I need continuous positive airflow or I could die."

I smiled and hugged him. [12]

---

[12] I screamed "I told you" for twenty minutes and remind him of my rightness weekly.

SUMMER OF THE BURRITO

My metabolism has slowed to a crawl. I've thought about getting all the fat sucked out of my "problem areas" because a girlfriend of mine had her muffin-top fat liposuctioned and her stomach looks amazing.

The problem with liposuction is that unless you give up burritos and everything delicious, the fat will return. Now, the fat can't return to the spot that has been liposuctioned because there are no fat cells there anymore, but the fat will come back SOMEWHERE. You would have to change your eating habits for life, and unfortunately, I have never met a burrito I didn't like. So, my burrito fat could return to the area above your belly button, which frankly is worse than a muffin-top. What if it settles in your neck or under your armpits? You can't Spanx your neck.

Regardless, I do support any and all procedures that make you look and feel better. Case in point, I pay to get my hair colored to cover the gray.

I've had my teeth straightened and I whiten them. Every night I use Retinol face cream. It's supposed to dry your face so that a layer of skin flakes off. Several times a week I use a "hydration mask" to put back some of the moisture the Retinol strips out.

Volcanic ash anti-aging mask

In the winter I get microdermabrasion, which is supposed to take off another layer of skin. Semiannually I get chemical peels. The solution they apply makes your skin blister and eventually fall off to reveal new, smoother, regenerated skin. Even with all the skin layers being removed and exfoliated I still have wrinkles, so I get Botox and fillers.

Potions and lotions

My friend, Carrie, and I were talking about all the money we spend on our faces and she asked me if I would ever invest over $10,000 to get a facelift because she was thinking about it. I told her the truth: We should just get boob jobs. If we had giant boobs, no one would notice our faces. She's taking my advice under consideration.

NICE TO MEET YOU

My friend, Marcia, [13] recently got divorced. She had been married for fifteen years when she discovered that her husband's business trips involved hookers and weed. After the appropriate mourning period, and at the urging of her sister, Marcia created an online dating profile.

The "dating profile," which all the sites recommend filling out, is supposed to allow people to get a glimpse into your character and hobbies. Marcia wrote a little bit about her family and said she was interested in someone who enjoyed traveling. She also mentioned that church was important in her life.

She is very beautiful and started getting the profiles of men that were interested in her right away. Although many of the applications were normal, listing a love of sports, allergies to cats, or a desire to visit Italy with a partner sometime soon, an exorbitant number of profile sections listed minimum requirements for certain attributes, such as "D-cup," or "Must like anal," or "No old chicks." Several guys stipulated: "Absolutely no hair, anywhere."

Marcia's stipulated age range was forty-five to fifty-five. You would think that "No hair" would not be a concern. What about good credit or no incurable STDs?

---

[13] Not her real name.

I understand people not wanting to waste time if someone has characteristics or personal habits that turn them off, such as smoking, but I'm suggesting they might save their anal-sex requirements for at least the third date.

Marcia went off-line for dating and online to get her master's degree. She ended up marrying a gentleman that she met in the organic vegetables section at Whole Foods. They are very happy and are currently putting in a koi pond.

PROCEED WITH CAUTION

I have OCD, four kids and a large dog. I mop incessantly. While I was cleaning, the TV commentators were discussing how the gravity-defying gymnast, Simone Biles, had changed the sport of gymnastics.

Simone Biles does midair twists while rotating in a different direction, with a blind landing, they explained. Other gymnasts had begun attempting more dangerous routines to have a shot at beating Simone. One vault routine, described by *The Wall Street Journal* as "one of the most daring of any event in the Olympic Games," is called the "vault of death." If you miss the landing, you will crack your neck, be paralyzed or possibly die. It's so dangerous even superstar Simone Biles said, "No thanks."

I left the living room to mop my bedroom for a few minutes, then returned to finish up in the mudroom when I heard the Olympic commentator say, "This event has left us confused and amazed." I rushed to the TV to see if Simone, or any of the other gymnasts had attempted something even more life-threatening. I was puzzled to see a synchronized swimming event.

I caught the end of the Russian team's routine, done to very dramatic "gladiators are coming for your heart" type music. The commentator yelled out, "EXPLOSIVE, BRILLIANT AND STAGGERING." A few swimmers were lifting another swimmer out of the water and flipping her. The routine was dynamic, but "explosive"? They showed clips of other routines and I thought one of the commentators was going to pop a vein. "They really do the unthinkable! Look at that synchronization!" And "It gives me goose bumps!"

I started mimicking the swimmers' moves, using my mop as my teammate, hoisting "her" up—but I slipped, in my socks, on the flip move. My mop whacked a glass lamp on the console table and I practically bit my tongue off as I crashed to the wet floor. As I considered the best way to get up without stepping on 1,000 pieces of broken glass, the commentators finished up.

"All of these young ladies wear nose plugs. If your nose plug comes off, I can guarantee it is painful and outright dangerous. But don't worry—these athletes, they hide an additional nose plug in their suits!"

This is a synopsis of "the medical aspects of synchronized swimming from the NCBI."

The most common injury in the sport of synchronized swimming is knee pain associated with the eggbeater kick.

I really appreciate the beauty and athleticism of these ladies, but for the record, since synchronized swimming became an Olympic event in 1968, no swimmer has ever had to be rescued from an eggbeater-kick injury. Mopping is more f****** dangerous.

THAT ONE TIME WHEN WE BOUGHT A PORSCHE

My car is from the last century, 1999 to be exact. I call it the Booger Wagon because I find actual boogers on the seats and even on the "ceiling." I asked my husband for a new car and he said, "It is not in the budget." I looked at the budget and saw that we have kids taking tennis lessons, kids taking equestrian lessons, some participating in after-school math programs and everyone going away to camps in the summer.

I decided that maybe some of the children didn't really need  camp and math tutoring. Having additional income, my husband surprised me with a Porsche 911. It is a very, very beautiful, high-performance car and he really liked it.

I know this sounds ungracious but I didn't want a Porsche 911. I'm forty-five and have four kids and wanted a white BMW 5 Series with tan interior and a sunroof. A convertible that goes 180 with a stick shift is not exactly practical. The problem with a Porsche 911 Carrera convertible is that you look like a crazed animal when you step out of it because the wind has beaten the s*** out of your hair and I already had accumulated lots of speeding tickets driving Hondas and Volkswagens let alone a Porsche. Did you know that going over 100 mph is considered "reckless driving," a charge that involves mandatory driver's education, a fine of over five hundred dollars and a $1,000 hike in your annual insurance premium?

Also, people treat me differently when I'm in the Porsche. In my booger wagon, with the four kids and golden retriever, people would smile and wave me over if I needed to change lanes. In the Porsche, if I hesitate for even a millisecond when the light turns green, people honk at me and scream, "Go, you a**hole!"

A Porsche is like a supermodel. A supermodel looks very beautiful but is expensive to maintain because she eats lots of caviar and wears Prada and Chanel. Seeing an older man with a Porsche or a supermodel always evokes the same reaction: "He must be a real douche."

After eighteen months, I told the hubby, "Let's sell the Porsche." We sold the 911 and got a used BMW 5 Series, white with tan interior, and a sunroof. I love it.

YOU'VE WON, STOP FIGHTING

I immediately drove the new-to-me white BMW 5 Series into the side of our garage. I have driven cars into many things: the spinning brushes at the carwash, my sister's minivan, my friend Kristin's vintage MG, and of course, mailboxes, poles and the like. After I swiped the side of the garage, I didn't even get out of the car; I drove to SSR Collision to see Tommy who fixes all the cars when I run into things.

What is unique about this particular mishap is that I barely scraped the paint but an entire chunk of bondo fell off the beautiful Certified Pre-Owned car, which launched us into a local, regional and eventual USA-headquarters battle with BMW.

Peter told me he would handle the situation, but I was so enraged about the injustice I refused his help. "We are not liable" was the dealership's position. Luckily, I could recite verbatim their Certified Pre-Owned Process-and-Procedures Guide and held my ground.

"It's impossible that you have completed the certification accurately AND did not find the damage AND now that you have been made aware of the damage you are still not responsible," I ranted. "It cannot be all three. Either you knew about the damage and didn't disclose it, as you are supposed to do as page six, paragraph three states in the pre-certification process, or you did not perform the pre-certification process checklist properly. Either way, you are liable."

Twenty-one days into battle, when my hair started coming out in chunks in the shower, I asked Peter to get involved.

I drove the booger wagon and Peter drove the bondo BMW to the dealership. Unfortunately, I got there first and went into a tirade with the regional vice president about how their "mission statement and values" were a total farce and, "God knows all the evil you are doing," before Peter drove in. I then excused myself to their fresh coffee and snack room. Within three minutes Peter came back out and told me I could pick out another car.

Peter explained the turn of events to me in terminology I would understand—Hollywood gossip-column talk. "Remember how Bill Cosby for over twenty years denied any wrongdoings regarding the sexual-misconduct cases filed against him?"

"Dear God, this is bigger than I expected."

"Pay attention," he said. "Bill Cosby said he wasn't liable, but quietly has paid out hundreds of thousands of dollars in 'tuition assistance' to women who have filed suits against him. You were so angry you never let them get past the 'We're not liable' statement and missed the 'But you can have a new car' offer."

The regional vice president came out and wanted to shake my hand. In my mind, I was reeling from the lying and smoke-and-mirrors politics, but when he said, "We'll find a white 5 Series with tan interior, a year newer," I said, "Thank you."

THE LORD, JESUS CHRIST

SHOCK: *Carrie Underwood's Husband Makes a MAJOR Confession*[14]

Typically, admissions in the world of tabloid news involve addiction, infidelity or embezzlement. But when Carrie Underwood's husband, Mike Fisher, said he was a Christian, it made headlines in the world of sensational news, as did this from actor Kevin Sorbo: "I don't know why in Hollywood you have to be afraid to say you're a Christian, but there's a lot of bashing of Christians going on over the last decade."[15]

You may be thinking, *You're damn right they should be afraid to admit to being Christian, the hypocritical lives they lead.* And I would say that I absolutely agree with you—and I'm a Christian! Christians have judged, criticized and excluded others for 2017 years. My only response is: I'M SO SORRY! And don't give up on faith because humans are reprehensible.

If you have the slightest curiosity about Christianity, Islam, Judaism, Buddhism, Hinduism or any religion, study their works before you dismiss them.

Briefly, I'll explain why I'm a believer. My personal thoughts (regarding the contents of the Bible) are that if someone were

---

[14]www.thepoliticalinsider.com/shock-carrie-underwoods-husband-makes-a-major-confession
[15]www.cnsnews.com/blog/mark-judge/kevin-sorbo-hollywood-you-have-be-afraid-say-youre-christian

trying to persuade another to believe in the promise of eternal life, they would make up a better story than following the teachings of a penniless carpenter conceived out of wedlock by a teenager. That's my reasoning: if it's all a lie, why wouldn't they make it a better lie?

The Bible is 1,200 pages of very unsavory stories. Jesus' bloodline is from prostitutes, thieves and murderers. Most the New Testament consists of letters (or books) that were written by the apostles (Jesus' selected teachers) while they were on the run from Roman authorities tasked to squash those involved with messianic movements.

All but two were murdered. Some were stabbed or speared (Matthew and Thomas), beheaded (James), skinned alive and then beheaded (Bartholomew), scourged then nailed (Philip) or tied to a cross (Andrew) to die. The other James (son of Alphaeus) was stoned then finished off with a club to his head. Peter was crucified on the cross upside down. Judas, who had betrayed Jesus, committed suicide. John was the only apostle to die of natural causes.

Do I have some questions about some of the content of the Bible? Yes. Do I think there is some wonky s*** in there? Yes. However, if you were lying to get people to invest into your idea, why wouldn't you present a more glamorous sales pitch? Consider the time-share: you are lured by "prestige and affordability" that are promised with free knives and toasters only to find out later that you are tethered to blackout dates and maintenance fees for life. In contrast, the Bible spells out that, as Christians, there will be "trouble" and "suffering" hundreds of times AND that Satan rules the earth. Plus, your reward doesn't come until after you die, and no toaster.

As I read the Bible, which exposes even the greatest of humans as so deeply flawed—David, a murderer; Solomon, with 700 wives and 300 concubines; Judas, the ultimate betrayer—I'm thinking, why would anyone make this up? It's so terrible.

The real message of the Bible, and of most religions, is to forgive and love others. If you are committed to a religion (any) and someone is trying to make you ashamed of it, you should tell them to f*** off. Bless their hearts.

YOU HAVE THE WRONG SUSPECTS

As a senior at Marietta High School in 1989, we were granted a few privileges. Only seniors had off-campus lunch, top-floor lockers and permission to leave school early for work. Toward the end of the year we celebrated Senior Week, Senior Snob Day and Senior Skip Day.

A non-school-endorsed tradition was the ritual of secretly re-painting the campus "rock," which sits at the top of a hill behind Marietta High. Officially, no one was allowed to alter the rock, but the administration would turn a blind eye for a big rival football game or end-of-the-year senior activities. So, when it came our turn, my girlfriends and I purchased our supplies and scheduled our covert painting operation with a few of our guy friends.

The guys didn't make an appearance until after we had finished, the giant rock now covered with our signature orange and black Tiger pride colors and giant letters spelling out:

Seniors Rule! 1989!

Wanting to take ownership of such a masterpiece, we had boldly signed our names—Amy, Kristin, Susan, Jenny, and Marilyn—in huge letters. The guys told us what a great job we had done, offered to carry all our supplies down the hill for us, and went off to do 360s in the now-empty school parking lot.

The next morning after the first bell rang, our principal, Mr. Malone, called our names over the loudspeaker, requesting that each of us "report to the office." Mr. Malone was a big supporter of school spirit, and we were thrilled to be called out of class, imagining a photo opportunity for us with the best senior rock ever.

That wasn't how it worked out. We huddled into chairs in front of Mr. Malone, his voice at once confirming the shockingly stern look we saw on his face. "Well, what do you girls have to say for yourselves?"

Marilyn was the first to speak up. She was a born leader and more confident than the rest of us since her father owned a string of sporting goods stores and had been a very generous donor to the football program over the years. "What are you talking about?" she said.

Mr. Malone raised the blinds on his office window and pointed outside where The Rock was clearly visible. It no longer read: "Seniors Rule! 1989!" Instead, to our horror, were the words:

Mr. Malone Sleeps Around!

Once again, Marilyn stepped up. "Mr. Malone, we did not paint that. We painted 'Seniors Rule.'"

Then Susan said, "We have pictures! Just let me take the film into the drug store, wait three to five days to get them developed and we'll show you!"

Silence. Mr. Malone looked out at The Rock, being prepped to paint by the janitor, then he looked at us in disappointment.

"You have made a mockery of this school and have set a bad example for Senior Week that can never be repaired," he said. "You have nothing else to say for yourselves?"

Long pause.

It was my turn. "Mr. Malone, we couldn't have painted that on The Rock. We didn't even know you were sleeping around."

Mr. Malone shot to his feet and shouted, "GET OUT OF MY OFFICE!" as he pointed at the door.

We were not further disciplined.

THE LOSER CRUISER

When I was in high school, the punished I dreaded the most was being restricted from driving the car and forced to ride the "loser cruiser" to school.

The only time the school bus was tolerable was when we were returning from a school athletic event, which could take several hours and was often shrouded in darkness, the perfect combination for trouble.

My sophomore year, while returning from a swim team trip, the seniors smuggled ten, two-liter glass bottles of Sun Country wine coolers in their swim bags. Sun Country, offering flavors such as tropical and peach and consisting of fruit juices, sugar and white wine, were the drink of choice for unsophisticated white women and high schoolers. The seniors were quite generous and shared their stash with the rest of us on the bus, a third of whom were freshmen. Most of us girls were new to booze, and many ended up getting very tipsy and making out with the junior and senior boys.

When the make-out session was disrupted by Mack Copeland,[16] whose drunken, bare-assed farts on sleeping teammates' faces turned into an accidental poop on Tyler Robbey, the coaches woke up and started asking what the hell what going on. In a panic, the seniors started chucking the Sun Country glass liters

---

[16] Not his real name.

out the bus windows. Police sirens ensued and the bus was pulled over.

Mack Copeland and the rest of boys were not punished for their roguery, but all the girls were kicked off the swim team and threatened with expulsion if we did not attend months of Alcoholics Anonymous meetings.[17]

I was also back on the yellow bus, restricted from driving the car.

---

[17] This story is a combination of two high school bus stories.

WORST BIRTHDAY EVER

I wish I had a *Sixteen Candles* type story of my own sixteenth birthday, one where the super-hot "Jake Ryan" was waiting for me at the end of a crappy day. But I don't. I celebrated my birthday at a bonfire, where my nemesis, Shana Moffit,[18] tried to kill me.

Shana and I were both "good" girls who had been elected to student council, played sports and wore tasteful outfits from The Limited or Ann Taylor. Shana, a foot taller and a year older than me, had been dating Marietta High School's version of Jake Ryan, Devin Trent.[19] Recently, though, I had started dating him. OK … "dating" would be a strong word; Devin and I hooked up after a night of playing beer pong at our buddy's condo and never "dated" again.

The night of my birthday party I was hoping to get back with an ex-ex-boyfriend, Sam, who was rumored to be coming to the bonfire. My girlfriends and I teased our spiral-permed hair into heights that would rival Marge Simpson's, reapplied a coat of black eyeliner and headed to the party.

Within minutes, Shana had spotted me and wanted to "talk about a few things." Normally I would have obliged because I was scared of her, but because it was my birthday and I had

---

[18] All names have been changed.

been sipping Boone's Farm[20] all night, I was a little cocky and told her, as nicely as I could, to go f*** herself. Shana was not used to such defiance and got eyelash to eyelash with me to express her disapproval regarding my hookup with Devin, the love of her life.

"Well, it seems you two have broken up," I said.

I was not prepared for her response. She started screaming obscenities and scratching my face with her very sharp acrylic nails. As she tried to "Mike Tyson"[21] me, I backed up, but in trying to escape I stumbled backwards over firewood and Shana landed on top of me. The crowd got really excited seeing two preppy chicks rolling on the ground. It looked like a full-throttle girl fight when really, I was just trying to push her off. A couple boys grabbed her, still kicking and screaming, and I headed home.

The following morning was the day of my actual birthday. My dad was mowing the grass. There were no presents. He had forgotten.[22]

---

[20] Cheap, fruity wine that teenagers drunk by the gallons.
[21] Bite my ear off.
[22] My dad made it up to me later with a trip to JCPenney.

COLLEGE LIFE

At Ohio State, I lived with five of the girls I had run around with in Marietta from junior high through graduation. It was the blind leading the blind. We got a house *off campus* on Indianola Street—in the ghetto. We walked to the Kroger that was predominantly supported by food stamps; thus, the price for a bunch of grapes was $9.50. However, it was within walking distance and they accepted our New Mexico fake IDs.

We had made our fake IDs with poster board, laminate and an iron, using alphabet stickers to change the name of each ID, but we were too lazy to change the address. When my high school posse showed up together at a bar at Ohio State, you would have thought the bouncers would be a tad bit suspicious: ten people whose names on their driver's licenses were Tara Coler, Kara Poler, Pam Cole, Tam Cole, Tim Cole, Tom Coler, Brin Cole, Brian Cole, etc., all with identical addresses in New Mexico. Miraculously, none of us ever had our fake IDs confiscated.

Anyway, our ghetto apartment in Columbus was less than twenty yards from a fire station, which made us feel much safer: a small price to pay for the sirens that went off incessantly, scaring our visitors to death and invoking lots of "What the f**k is that?"

Our neighbors were a group of cute boys, also OSU students, who were paying their way through college as drug dealers. None of us suspected a thing, despite the fact that all night long we could hear people coming and going, ringing their doorbell or knocking.

It was 1991, and Nancy Reagan's War on Drugs was still in full swing: it was not unusual for antidrug protesters to march down our street with *Just Say No* signs. One Tuesday night the sirens were not from the fire station, but from a police raid with officers wielding warrants and busting drug dealers. In clear view of our windows we could see the nice boys next door being escorted out in handcuffs, never to be seen again.

JUST SAY NO

I've been lucky enough, if that is even the right term, to have never been swayed into doing drugs, though my hometown was less than an hour from the weed capital, Meigs County, famous for its *Meigs County Gold*. I was never into pot and was not exposed to any other drugs until I went away to college.

At Ohio State there were two, twenty-three-story dormitories, Morrill and Lincoln Towers. On campus, they were referred to as "The Towers." The most famous resident of The Towers was Jeffrey Dahmer, the mass murderer. He lived on the fifth floor of Morrill Tower in 1978 for less than one academic quarter.

My dad lived in Lincoln Tower in the 1960s, and not much had changed in thirty years. Each suite crammed sixteen kids into four bedrooms, one bathroom and a tiny living room, complete with orange shag carpet. Pack over 1,000 eighteen-year-old kids into one building and you get what you would expect: a 24/7 spring-break environment and a drop-out rate of over 50 percent.

A few guys from my high school lived in The Towers and invited my lady squad to hang out. After about an hour, with twenty people crowded into the living room, drinking Schlitz, a wait began to grow for the bathroom. Two guys suggested we head next door to their suite to use their bathroom, if we wanted. "The door was open."

We knocked, then let ourselves in. Several girls started screeching. The draft from opening the door had blown the cocaine they had been snorting off the glass coffee table into a fog. The girls were waving their arms around trying to capture the floating powder and snorting the cocaine off the thirty-year-old orange shaggy carpet. I knew that drugs were not for me.

I AM OLD. I LIKE FACEBOOK

I like the extremes of the posts. The optimists: *Make today a great day!* 😊 and the pessimists: *My cholesterol levels are still too high, another doctor's appointment today.* ☹️

It may seem silly that I spend so much time on Facebook looking at videos of kids trying to talk after they have had their wisdom teeth yanked out of their heads, but it gives me a reprieve from laundry and having to have sex with my husband.

My favorite FB posts are guinea pigs in outfits, toddlers dancing to Michael Jackson, people falling, baby otters squeaking while lying on their mama otters' bellies, bunny rabbits and puppies snuggling with other animals like birds, lions and cats. *ADORABLE!*

The *I'm better than you!* posts are annoying. *We are blessed that Julie has college scholarship offers from Yale and Brown! Look at my new Mercedes S Class! We are eating at a restaurant that none of you can afford!* We used to be subjected to those sorts of announcements only once a year, getting the obnoxious gloating Christmas letters; now we're bombarded daily.

Facebook demands are the worst: *If you love Jesus, you will like and share this post. If you do not share this post, you do not love Jesus*, or *I want to see who is reading my posts, so leave a word that starts with P and then cut and paste onto your own timeline. DO NOT JUST SHARE! If you share, I'm going to know you did not read the post and you are not my friend.*

I have a word that starts with the letter P for these people ... P-r-o-z-a-c. If you need that much attention, get a puppy. Facebook is supposed to be recreational so quit bossing me. ☺

AMY AND ANNA GO TO CHINA

Recently, my daughter and I went to China to visit my friend Kristin. Flights to China are expensive, thus I kept playing with the arrival and departure dates until I saw a fare I could live with. I informed Kristin that we would be staying for eighteen days. I realize that eighteen days is overstaying a welcome by about twelve days, but Kristin is very polite and replied, "Great!"

There are many myths about China.

Myth	TRUE	FALSE	DETAIL
The food is bad.		x	The food is different. They have over a billion people to feed. They eat snakes, frogs, silkworms, sea horses, baby duck embryos, turtles, cats and dogs.
Everybody smokes.		x	But the people that do smoke, do so incessantly—even while they are eating dinner.
The people are mean.		x	The people are aggressive.
They're horrible drivers.	x		Kristin's advice: "Close your eyes."
Everything is cheap.		x	Housing is extremely expensive. Purchasing an imported car will cost you an additional 50 percent in taxes.
They hate Americans.		x	The Chinese people love Americans. The Great Wall has a sign that reads "Welcome American Tourists."

Statement			Explanation
China's hard to navigate around.	x		If you cannot read Chinese symbols, it's difficult.
Everybody has servants.	x		It is customary for ex-pats to employ multiple Chinese people in their homes, such as a chef, groundskeeper and housekeepers.
You could be thrown in jail at any minute.	x		China is a Communist country.
There's a lot of crime.		x	The punishments for any crimes are severe.
They have a drug problem.		x	Drugs are everywhere in the world but China's punishment for drug-trafficking is execution by firing squad.
Only one child per family is allowed.		x	The law has been overturned.
China smells.	x		People apply Tiger Balm ointment under their noses to mask the smells.
China's dirty.		x	It depends on where you are; tourist areas are kept clean.
You may die if you get sick in China.	x		Quality healthcare is very difficult to find.
You potty in a hole.	x		The toilet bowl is flush with the ground. You squat. Higher-end places offer both sitting and squatting toilets.
You must travel with wipes.	x		Most facilities in China do not offer soap, toilet paper or paper towels.
You should visit China.	x		Hire a guide and you will have an amazing trip.

Kristin lives in Beijing, "The Buckhead of China," I tell her. (Buckhead is a swanky area of Atlanta.) She lives in a gated community with neighbors that are industry executives for Volkswagen and BMW and embassy people from around the world. While I was visiting, she invited me to her book club, which club was held at a six-hundred-year-old converted temple located in the Dongcheng District. The restaurant logo is below:

I thought it was a translation error: "They are really dumbing this down for the Americans, calling it the 123," but those are the initials "TRB" for Temple Restaurant Beijing. The lovely lunch included outstanding service, appetizers, main courses, several desserts and many bottles of wine. My bill was $28, including the tip.

There is such a dichotomy of income in China. Just outside Kristin's neighborhood one can see peasant men sitting on buckets selling live snapping turtles (suspended from fishing poles) while men wearing Armani suits are driving along in Ferraris. Although China is officially Communist, they have a somewhat capitalistic economy.

Kristin is an outstanding shopping guide, as she SPEAKS MANDARIN FLUENTLY and has exquisite taste (more on that later). My favorite part of the trip was checking out the local markets, filled with artists and their handmade wares, like boxes made of tiles from 1,000-year-old temples, and Chinese molds used to make mooncakes, the traditional cookies baked for special occasions like the Mid-Autumn Festival, when the full moon and moon gazing are celebrated. To make the cakes, wooden paddles are hand-carved into different mold designs of fish, symbolizing surplus or good fortune; ducks, for a happy marriage; and flowers, for wealth.

Fish design mold and cookies

While we were at the market, Kristin bought a fantastic hand-carved Buddha. Her driver, Mr. Chan, respectfully secured him in the passenger seat.

In addition to the handmade boxes and mooncake molds, there were beautiful hand-crafted, painted umbrellas; hand-carved

buddhas; and handmade paper painted with plum blossoms, the national flower of the Republic of China. The flower blooms in the midst of winter, providing a beautiful reminder that spring is coming, and symbolizes resilience and perseverance in the face of adversity. If you've studied Chinese history, you recognize that they have had their fair share of adversity.

AMY AND ANNA ARE STILL IN CHINA

We also visited the Great Wall. Normally, the pollution is so bad you cannot see from one tower to the next, but we were fortunate enough to be there on one of the clearest days they'd had in months, and it was magnificent. As I was enjoying a moment of complete majestic-ness, David (Kristin's husband) informed me that the Great Wall is also called "The Longest Cemetery on Earth" because the remains of a million soldiers, peasants and criminals who were worked to death are "buried" in the wall.

Photographs portray the wall as winding and gentle, but climbing it you realize there are also very steep areas. We climbed portions of the wild wall—sections that had not been repaired. As all the children and some in our group headed back down on a lift, I stayed and slowly scaled a segment that was practically straight up with very narrow, razor-sharp rocks. As I struggled to the top—hot, exhausted, and with knees bloodied—I could see the tower was only a few more yards. I willed myself to keep going. Holding back tears, I finally slapped my arm up on the tower floor and pulled myself up.

I was greeted by what sounded like "Cock for you? Cock?" In the tower was a 100-year-old toothless Chinese man sitting crisscross-applesauce style wearing a RUN DMC shirt selling ice-cold Cokes from his cooler. Of course, I didn't have any cash, so he hustled me out like I was a yard chicken.

Entertaining guests for eighteen days allows time for a weekend trip. For five hundred dollars, we hopped on a plane and booked a hotel and an English-speaking tour guide to show us around Xi'an for two days. Xi'an (pronounced shee-an) is one of the four Ancient City great capitals and one of the oldest cities in China. The first day we enjoyed a ten-mile bike tour on the original city wall (built in 194 BC), visited an art museum, and had dinner in town. I fell about seven times. Everything is very slippery in China, as if they are trying to reduce the population with slip and falls.

I never got used to people being allowed to smoke in restaurants. We sat next to a group of four Chinese gentlemen that were intermittently smoking and eating. For a country where the average weekly income is less than $100, It's surprising to see Chinese people spending their resources on cigarettes.

We spent the night in a nice, modern hotel and were picked up by a driver and guide first thing in the morning to explore Emperor Qinshihuang's Mausoleum Site Museum, home to the incomparable terracotta warriors.

At the site are four buildings, each with a pit that displays eight thousand uniquely designed terracotta warriors with their weapons, horses and chariots, plus acrobats, strongmen and musicians. The buried grounds cover thirty-eight square miles and were originally covered with elaborately carved roofs and then covered with soil.

Why are thousands of handmade terracotta sculptures buried with the emperor? The net of the story is as follows: The first emperor of China wanted the warriors to protect him in the afterlife. His still very-much-alive concubines were also buried with him (at his request) in his tomb. The emperor's actual tomb has NOT been excavated as archaeologists have said they do not have the proper technology to explore it. The grounds of the tomb are also immersed with poisonous mercury, believed to "promote immortality." A farmer in the 1970s found a piece of one of the warriors when he was digging a well and the rest is history—really, really old history.

In every tourist-rich area we visited, my daughter, Anna, was an attraction. She's pale, tall and has bright, white-blond hair—a combination not often seen in China. Up to six people at a time, especially teenage girls and old ladies, would ask if they could photograph her. "Photo? Photo?" they would ask. Anna was thrilled. Parents would make their kids stand by her, which Chinese boys did not find thrilling.

Anna's other favorite part of our trip was when Kristin's hubby, David, would drive Anna and their two girls around in the Tut-tut. David's company does not allow anyone in his household to drive, hence they have Mr. Chan. When Mr. Chan is off, they take the Tut-tut.

Tut-tut

When you have over a billion-people living in the country, there is a lot of traffic, noise and pollution. One advantage to having a billion people is the affordability of services. Kristin, her best friend Kimberly, Anna and I enjoyed going to a salon and getting a luxurious Chinese shampoo. The attendant washed and massaged our heads with minty conditioner for over forty minutes followed by a neck massage and blow dry. Our bill was $20.

Anna getting a neck massage and blow dry.

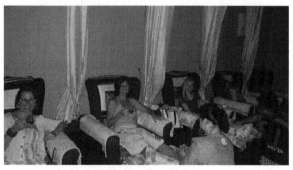

Kristin, Anna and I enjoying foot massages and green tea.

An hour-long foot massage served with snacks and tea also cost around $20. No wonder Kristin looks so amazing.

AMY AND ANNA ARE WEARING OUT THEIR WELCOME IN CHINA

My final adventure in China was the shopping mall. Getting there was an undertaking in itself. Although Mr. Chan is an outstanding driver, Chinese drivers are very aggressive and have no regard for lines on the roads, stop signs or, frankly, human life. Kristin's advice, as I mentioned in the chart earlier, is to "close your eyes."

After about an hour, we arrived at what looked like an American shopping mall, complete with clothing stores; a food court with Pizza Hut and Starbucks; a wholesale section with Chinese fans, electronics, and T-shirts; and a Pear Market, where famous people such as Barbara Bush had shopped. Other floors offered cashmere sweaters and traditional Chinese kimonos.

As you walk in the market the Chinese sales girls say, "Lady, lady, lady," trying to get you to stop and shop at their booths. Prices are negotiable, and just like a yard sale, the more you act like you want it, the higher the price. The instant the sales girls heard Kristin speaking Mandarin, the sales girls dropped the prices and said, "Best sale."

I picked up several packs of chopsticks for the kids ($1/ten-pack) and bought thirty adorable nightshirts printed with Chinese symbols ($3/piece). Next, we hit the "knock-knock" stores. To my delight, I was introduced to the black market within the walls of the shopping mall.

It went down like this: Kristin would text a vendor on her phone and wait for a reply of a location. Once the location came in, we'd head to whatever floor the group was on. The black-market vendors moved around a lot because the police often raided them. We would wait by a door, in a random hallway, and knock—hence the nickname "knock-knock." A Chinese lady would peek out and hustle us into what looked like a broom closet, complete with buckets and mops. We would step over the mops and follow the woman down a winding hall to another door. She'd open the door and voila! You were now standing in a room of counterfeit Prada bags.

It was like Rodeo Drive except you had to step over the mops, negotiate with aggressive Chinese people and risk being arrested at any minute. Other than that, it was MAGICAL. I felt like Julia Roberts in *Pretty Woman* after the saleswoman refused to wait on her and Richard Gere took her to the nicest shops in LA and told the shop manager he was going to be spending "really obscene" amounts of money and all the salespeople fell all over her—ordering her pizza and giving her their neckties right off their necks.

Imagine Burberry, Hermes, Lululemon, Cartier, Prada, Gucci and Tiffany's—all 90 percent off. Most of the salespeople knew Kristin and her friends by name and could speak a little English. I walked into a scarf store by myself and asked about a few items when Kristin's friend Cheryl, from Dallas, walked in and said to the salesperson, "No, no, no—show her the good stuff." The saleslady greeted her and walked me to what looked like a makeup bag display, cleared off the makeup bags and opened the display up, like a Transformer figure, revealing beautifully organized "Chanel" scarves.

Returning to America with my stolen or counterfeit goods was so exciting. I gifted all my girlfriends bags and scarves. Within weeks one mentioned that their Louis Vuitton(ish) wallet was falling apart. All I could muster was, "No shit, it's made in China.

CALL FROM SHARON
THE SHE'S A WHORE CALL

Sharon: Oh my god, he married that whore!

Me: Who?

Sharon: Mike,[23] the hottest guy in Buffalo.

Me: Who?

Sharon: Mike Parnell! I saw him at the reunion. He had lost his wife—brain aneurysm. Cooking a grilled cheese one minute and then dead on the floor the next. It makes me so mad. She's a gold-digging whore.

Me: That's terrible.

Sharon: Yes. She was a lovely woman, but this new one is a skank. She came on to Scott in the elevator! She totally insinuated that she enjoys anal sex. And Mike MARRIED her. The salami looks dry.

Me: Sorry?

Sharon: I'm at the grocery store—the deli's picked over. The man had just lost his wife for hell's sake. She started delivering casseroles and pastries—you know her mother was Greek—she thinks her melomakarona[24] is all that. The woman has never

---

[23] Names changed.

[24] www.food.com/recipe/melomakarona-a-greek-christmas-cookie

worked a day in her life. She seduced him with baked goods. She's a tramp and wants her hands on his pension from the post office!

Me: Men replace, women rebuild.

Sharon: They are slicing new salami. Anyway, make sure that your girls go to a solid college and get good jobs. You don't want them winding up divorced, with no skills and having to be sexual deviants to land a husband. Click.

ANTI-SOCIAL MEDIA

A few months ago, it was the clown hoax. All four of our children were reporting that their schools were on Code Red due to the "clown situation." The clown hysteria started on Instagram with posts: Reports of clowns *luring children into the woods and murdering them*. It escalated to major news outlets: *Clown Phobia, Scary and Menacing Clowns, and Terrorizing Clown Sightings*. Police issued warnings about the *Killer Clown Attack*s.

In Ohio, schools were closed for the *safety of the students*. In Georgia, parents were getting notifications stating that *No clowns would be admitted to the schools, for ANY reason*.

An armed-clown hoax temporarily put a Massachusetts college on lockdown.

Hundreds of students in Pennsylvania State University swarmed surrounding campus streets to carry out a *mass clown hunt*. A Connecticut school district said it is *banning* clown costumes and any *symbols of terror*.

The hoax was rumored to be a marketing ploy by a fiction writer for an upcoming horror film. However, some clowns were spotted armed with appropriately terrifying weapons: In New York, a knife-wielding *jerk in clown makeup* chased a teen out of a subway. And a clown recently sighted at a London university was said to have been *toting a chainsaw*.[25]

The clown hoax did take a toll on the professional clown community. Jordan Jones, who works part-time portraying Snuggles the Clown in a haunted house, said, "I fear for my life."[26] A clown from Naperville reported to the *Chicago Tribune*, "They say there's a shortage of clowns. I hope this doesn't scare people away."[27]

Times are tough all over.

---

[25] www.mic.com/articles/156482/clown-sightings-2016-here-s-what-real-clowns-are-saying-about-the-killer-clown-hoax#.IrJM95tG2

[26] www.time.com/4518456/scary-clown-sighting-attack-craze

[27] www.chicagotribune.com/suburbs/naperville-sun/news/ct-nvs-impact-creepy-clowns-st-1012-20161011-story

JOHN D. BINEGAR

My dad is almost eighty and still works forty hours a week for a telecommunications company. He says he doesn't have the temperament for golf so he may as well work. He's like the mayor of my hometown.

Dad comes and visits us in Atlanta, from Ohio, twice a year. He promises to stay a week, but he never lasts more than two nights. The first day he outlines what happened on his 500-mile route to Atlanta. "I hate that I-85. It always gets backed up with road work going through Charlotte. Added an hour to the trip."

The second day we drag him to the kids' tennis matches and horse shows—the kids arguing with us and each other—so by dinner he's planning his escape. "I really need to get back to work. I'll just head up I-75 north, then to 64 and cut over toward Huntington, everything except the West Virginia Turnpike has really good roads."

My dad holding me.

He also likes to tell stories completely mispronouncing words and people's names.[28] "It is so awful about that Bill 'Crosby' fellow who played the doctor on TV. He seemed like a real stand-up guy. He's had sex with so many women he probably has the 'herbes.'"

The road signs in Georgia infuriate my father because frankly, they don't make sense. Georgia 20 is also called Buford Highway. Jimmy Carter Boulevard suddenly turns into Holcomb Bridge Road, with no warning. Going downtown is a disaster because there are seventy-one roads with variants of Peachtree. "What kind of deranged bureaucrat names these damn roads?" At first I tried to defend Georgia's roads, but things go better if I join the outrage. I throw out a "That is ridiculous! Why would they do such a thing?"

When I call my dad, he tells me about the weather, particularly rain, because that dictates how many times he has to mow his grass. He calls me to ask why Ohio State is losing football or basketball, depending on the season, as if, because OSU is my alma mater, I have some sort of influence on the Big Ten.

We recently started texting one another. So far, he's texted me weather reports, his interest in attending a roller derby match and his feedback about his visit to Israel. "Israel's hot and all they want to talk about is Jesus, Jesus, Jesus."

My dad gave me great advice, I just wasn't listening.

1. Money is not important until you need it, then it becomes very important.

2. Always buy the best that you can afford.

---

[28] I have inherited this issue. See page 12.

3. Drink water constantly. From stomachaches to heartbreak, water is the solution.

4. Exercise every day.

5. Don't shoot your mouth off. This may be a southern Ohio adaptation of James 1:19: *My dear brothers and sisters, take note of this: Everyone should be quick to listen, slow to speak and slow to become angry.*

6. Don't become an idiot. Read something or do a crossword for Christ's sake.

7. If you have time to lean, you have time to clean. (Borrowed from Roy Kroc, founder of McDonald's)

8. Don't try because you can't change f****** people.

9. Think *Would my grandmother do this?* before you do something. It's a twist on *What Would Jesus Do?* but my dad said it first.

10. A word to the wise is sufficient, but you're not wise; you are a dumbass, that's why I'm telling you again. The first part of this saying is Yiddish. I'm not sure where he picked it up,[29] but the dumbass part is definitely his own.

My dad's the salt of the earth and the epitome of his era, loving John Wayne, Elvis and firearms.

---

[29] I grew up in a town of white Protestants.

IF YOU TEACH A MAN TO FISH

Peter grew up in downtown Atlanta. His father had been a vice president for a large food corporation and then had a second career as a college professor. His mother had her own nurse anesthetist firm. Peter grew up *with* help—a nanny and a housekeeper—and his family had a membership to a country club. I was the first person in my family to finish college, and I worked as a nanny and a waitress, so I *was* the help.

Being a southern gentleman, Peter shocked me the first year we were married when he announced he was "going hunting." Deer hunting in my small town was often done out of necessity. Even if you ran over a deer in my hometown, someone would pick it up—to cook and eat.

Deer hunters in my hometown carry their rifles on gun racks, attached to their pickup trucks and head "to the hollows." They wear camouflage head-to-toe and carry coolers filled with Pabst Blue Ribbon purchased from Walmart. Hunters sprinkle scents made from head and hoof glands of the deer plus lady deer urine around the area. They sit in deer stands to drink and wait. If they kill a deer they throw it on their pickup trucks and take it home to "process."

I have Christmas cards from my cousins featuring their children on the back of a pickup truck holding up the head of a dead buck with the caption "First kill! Merry Christmas!"

Peter informed me he was quail hunting at Burge Plantation, which is listed on the National Historic Registry and offers 1,000 acres of sporting and hunting grounds. People arrive wearing thousands of dollars' worth of Filson hunting apparel, equipped with fine Italian Beretta rifles. Members and guests warm up by shooting skeet, then are greeted by their hunting guides and highly trained Chesapeake Bay Retrievers. They proceed to fields where earlier that morning the guides had hand planted domestically raised quail and pheasants into Burge's bushes. The guides shake the bushes, the birds fly out and the hunt begins.

After the hunt, the group enjoys lunch and Cuban cigars at a million-dollar clubhouse. Upon departure, the hunters are handed custom coolers that have completely cleaned birds encased in thick plastic freezer bags.

Thank goodness Peter has a very generous uncle that invites him on an annual trip.

Peter says he enjoys hunting and fishing regardless where the activity is taking place and that "the best things in life are free." Billionaire Apple founder, Steve Jobs, said something similar: "My favorite things in life don't cost any money." I bet he said that after he bought a $120 million super yacht that he would fly to on his own private jet. I enjoy a sunset as much as the next person, but I think people that say that money is not important already have a lot of it.

QUEEN GENEVIEVE

My hometown, Marietta, Ohio, is nestled alongside the Ohio River. The Seneca Indians occupied the territory as early as 1492 and named the river "Ohio," which means "It is beautiful." Fact: the Ohio River bordering Marietta is owned by West Virginia. A Deed of Concession set the river as the western boundary back when West Virginia was just Virginia. The river, even though they don't own it, is Marietta's most important asset as several manufacturing plants use the river water to cool their industrial equipment and it is an attraction for tourists.

For one weekend in September, Marietta's population of 10,000 explodes to over 100,000 with visitors for the Sternwheel Festival. The weekend features sternwheel boats, live bands, an impressive firework show shot off a river barge and an announcement of the "Queen Genevieve" pageant.

The Queen Genevieve contestants model and answer a few questions, after which the scores are "calculated by a local accounting firm." I'm not sure why an accounting firm is necessary for the "calculation" of the Queen Genevieve scores, as most years there are normally only five contestants, four of whom receive awards: Queen Genevieve, Runner-up to Queen, Miss Congeniality, and Committee's Choice.

The winners of the Queen Genevieve contest get up to $1,500 in scholarship money toward the local county community college.

My parents refused to let me try out for the Queen Genevieve pageant, saying it was "all political." But I bet it was because I had thin hair and a slight overbite.

In 2014 *Smithsonian* magazine listed Marietta as one of the best small towns to visit. They mentioned the highlights as the Sternwheel Festival followed by the Sweet Corn Festival.

I have never attended, but the Sweet Corn Festival features the sale of over 6,000 ears of corn and a feed-corn-bag-tossing tournament, in case you are interested.

WE HAVE A SITUATION

A group of girls and I went to see the coolest '80s band in concert. I can't name them because I would have to pay royalties and I don't want anyone to think my idea of an '80s band is lame, so I have left it up to you, the reader, to insert your own favorite band. The concert was held at Chastain Park Amphitheatre, an outdoor venue with tables. You can bring your own food and enjoy a picnic, unless the artist is James Taylor. James was shocked that people were slicing their cheese and serving wine while he was performing. He stopped the concert and demanded that everyone take their coolers back to their cars. He kept screaming, "I am not background music for your dinner!"

The '80s band was cool and seemed to enjoy an audience filled with picnickers. Our group had brought a strange combination of foods including a variety of cheeses, fruit, boxes of tacos, Krystal burgers and Thai chicken skewers.

Approximately fifteen seconds before the intermission, my stomach started to percolate at an alarming level. I was sweating and doing contraction-type breathing. Sharon, recognizing my irritable bowel symptoms as we have the same sensitive stomachs, headed to the bathroom with me, repeating, "Just breathe … It's okay … We're almost there," as we fought our way through thousands of people making a rush for the beer lines.

Fortunately, the combination of being bent over in pain and taking short breaths while Sharon counted "Good, one, two, three," caused people to assume I was going into labor and the way was cleared for me.

When I finally made it into a stall, Sharon, hovering outside the door, asked, "How's it going in there, honey?"

Humiliated, I had to admit, "I'm fine, but I had to throw away my panties." Sharon tried not to giggle.

The next morning at nine, I had a tennis match on our home courts. As I walked up to the pavilion with my tennis bag, Meg, my neighbor (surrounded by eight or nine of our opponents) said, "Hey, I heard about the concert."

I almost ran but decided to face my humiliation head-on. "That's right. I have an illness. I had a lot of cheese and wine and several Thai skewers and I pooped my pants."

The opponents fled. Meg and I stood staring at each other for several seconds before she said, "I only had heard it was an awesome concert."

"Oh. It was totally cool." I picked up my tennis bag and headed to the courts.

CALL FROM SHARON
THE PLUTO CALL

Sharon: Inaudible ... Bailey! ... Inaudible ... phone drops. Bailey! (Sharon's dog) Shit! Hello!

Me: Sharon—I'm here.

Sharon: What?

Me: I'm here!

Sharon: Oh, good. Blake got a C on his f****** science project because Pluto is now a planet!

Me: Pluto is a planet.

Sharon: No, it has NOT always been a planet. It was a celestial body. It orbits the sun but doesn't do some other s*** worthy of a planet. I know this because a few years ago, when we did Ty's project, I too, thought Pluto was a planet and he got a C because the teachers said Pluto WAS NOT a planet. Bailey, come here! Bailey! No! But now it is a planet! BAILEY! I have to go.

Click.

APOCALYPTIC THOUGHTS

I live in a midsize neighborhood north of Atlanta. We have our own webpage designed to "promote community," marketed as a way for people to find last-minute babysitters and lost pets and to report which restaurants failed health inspections. But most the posts are neighbors ratting out their own neighbors for dogs pooping in their yards, kids driving too fast on golf carts and "solicitors on the loose."

For a time, a group of families moved in that were rumored to be members of the Endtime Ministries cult. People started posting article links about how the Endtime ladies couldn't wear makeup because of the "lipstick spirit" and the men could not have facial hair because of the "homosexual spirit." Holidays, even Christmas and Easter, were banned as "pagan rituals" and nobody ever saw an Endtimer with a pet because they thought of animals as "harbored demons."

Coincidentally when the three rumored cult families moved in, neighborhood pets—several dogs, but especially neighborhood cats—started disappearing. It did seem strange that "LOST CAT" postings were appearing almost daily in our small community. People started pointing fingers at the cult members. More and more posts appeared about rumored strange doings of the Florida Endtimers, including killing animals, tax fraud, the handling of snakes and forced underage marriages.

The final posts regarding the cult/cat issue on our neighborhood site:

"I am concerned that the Endtime Ministries cult members are engaging in some sort of cat extermination mission, as now more than four cats have been reported missing and zero have been recovered."

Many people replied. This was my favorite:

"This very thing happened in our last neighborhood so we had to teach the cats to fight."

It seems no hurt feelings resulted from these neighborhood exchanges because the Endtimers didn't sign up for the community website. They believe that media—newspapers, radio, television, the Internet—are instruments of demons.

Still no word on the cats.

RANT: EVERYBODY'S A PROFESSIONAL

None of my children won any of these ribbons

My husband and I were encouraging our eighth grader, PJ, to try out for the golf team. PJ vehemently said he wasn't good enough. He was right. Half of the middle-school boys competing for the team had handicaps of *zero*. In the world of golf, that is crazy good; less than one percent of golfers in the world achieve such a status.

What's happening in kids' sports?

You used to be able to put your kid on the YMCA recreational team and if they had talent, which may have been identified in middle school, they would move up. Recreational teams are becoming more and more scare. The message seems to be "if your kid isn't on a travel team, they're not good."

It's the industry of … the travel team. "Elite" team sports are a 7-billion-dollar business and everybody's doing it. In Minnesota, there were 23 basketball travel teams in 1991, now there are 1,400.[30]

A *Forbes* magazine study reported that parents are spending boatloads of money (many exceed $1,000 a month) hoping it will pay off in a lucrative athletic career.[31] Kids as young as seven now play year-round in what were once seasonal sports.

Athletes don't get a break over the holidays either—they attend agility, velocity, or conditioning camps. For football, they offer Passing and Receiving Academies and/or the Kicking and Long-Snapping Camp taught by ex-NFL players. If your kids play soccer, they could attend *Campamentos de Fútbol* in Italy, Portugal, Spain or France.

The investment is not paying off. Only 5 percent of the eight million high school athletes even make it to the college level, let alone pro. The odds for going pro: 1 in 11,771 for basketball, 1 in 5,768 for soccer and 1 in 4,233 for football.

Did I make a terrible mistake by letting my kids try different sports? Have I failed because I didn't identify my kid's athletic strengths by the time they were toddlers? Yes, because not one of the four has been able to make ANY team sport whatsoever. All our children have rotated in and out of out of soccer, karate, dance, equestrian lessons, football and tennis.

Our kids will play a pickup game of soccer or kickball in the park and they're developing skills in backyard game of corn hole.

As of yet no scholarship offers have come in.

---

[30] www.minnesota.cbslocal.com/2015/11/16/as-competition-rises-team-sports-decline-but-traveling-teams-soa

[31] www.forbes.com/sites/bobcook/2016/08/01/what-drives-parents-youth-sports-spending-dont-underestimate-peer-pressure

WALMART IS AMERICA

When you go to Walmart, you know what you're getting. The parking lots are peppered with beat-up, late-model cars that have cardboard for windows and that drag exhaust pipes that scream *Welcome to hell.*

On one trip, I tried to locate the special Birthday Wishes Barbie to no avail. When I asked the stockperson where I could locate the Birthday Barbie, she replied, "No much English."

I asked, "Is there someone that does speak English that could help me?"

She held up four fingers and I believe she said, "Not until four o'clock."

As a mom of four, I do a monthly Walmart trip because milk, orange juice, cereal and cleaning supplies are a dollar cheaper than in grocery stores. Furthermore, you can pick up one of the best wines in the under-$15 range for only $12—or even cheaper if you buy the case. It's not milk; it doesn't spoil.

Walmart employs over one percent of the United States population.[32] I look at the employees who get up every day and put on their blue vests to work for minimum wage and realize how in the United States, most people are trying ... and that's honorable.

---

[32] www.businessinsider.com/walmart-employees-pay

WE'RE OUTNUMBERED

We have four teenagers in our house ranging from age thirteen to eighteen. Children ask an inexhaustible number of questions:

- Can I sleep over at Jill's Friday?
- Can Gabby, Katie, Alexis and Emma sleep over on Saturday?
- Why can't I get a new phone/sneakers/dress/video game/rug for my room?
- Did you drink alcohol in high school?
- Will you look at this lump on my cheek/leg/arm?
- Why can't I go to the Bahamas for spring break with my friend?
- What is the difference between whole milk, skim milk, 2 percent milk and almond milk?
- Why do we have to go X to eat? I want to go to Y.
- Why isn't (sibling) grounded too?
- Why can't I get a tattoo of Coldplay lyrics on my forearm?
- When can I have my phone back? When can I have my phone back? When can I have my phone back?

That's why Peter says, "Ask your mother," and I say, "Ask your father." We're tired.

The three girls have an incessant need for argon oil for their hair or Naked eyeshadow pallets, Micro-delivery Face Exfoliating Creams and those Cut-for-Chuck Taylor's tiny socks that don't show when you wear Converse sneakers and never appear again once you put them into the washer. The boy wants things

100

that require batteries like the Shadowhawk x800 Military Tactical Flashlight and flying drones that can take videos.

The three things that the children never ask for are underwear, toothpaste and toilet paper. We could be on vacation, several weeks in, and I'll ask all four to "show me your toothbrushes." At least two of them can't. There are always lots of pants, shirts and shorts, in the laundry but very few pairs of underwear. They have bathrooms, but no toilet paper. I no longer inquire about the underwear or toilet paper because all four answer the exact same way: "I don't know."

We have one recently licensed driver and two permitted drivers. Our car insurance is approaching mortgage levels. The kids drive an inherited Tahoe and its once-rectangular shape is now rounded due to the kids crashing into things.

We make Savannah, the licensed driver, chauffeur her three siblings around and have been getting complaints about their experiences as passengers. "She drives super-fast even if it's raining or if there are a bunch of orange cones." When her brother, PJ, told her to slow down, she told him to "shut it" because she was "the only person in the car that has a driver's license."

When I asked Savannah about the dangerous driving, she gave me the same response she had given her brother: "They don't have their driver's licenses so how would they know if I was doing anything wrong?"

I tried to appeal to her logically: "If we were in a plane and it started hurling toward the ground … I'm not a pilot but I know something is not right."

Regardless of what we are asking our children to do, they have two go-to responses" "Well, that's your opinion," and "At least I'm not on heroin."

Oftentimes it's a combination of the two. I'll say, "You need to be responsible for your own room; you are a citizen of this house." They reply, "That's your opinion. At least I'm not doing heroin."

People who say they don't believe in spanking have never spent time with our children.

NO NEED TO SHARE EVERYTHING

At dinner one night, our middle daughter, Maddy, who is seventeen, shared that she had tried strawberry-flavored vodka at a party and "really liked it." I have mixed feelings about our kids confessing their sins to us. It does create an opportunity for discussion, but also brings about nonstop worry.

For my husband's birthday, we had a (grown-ups only) seventies party. My girlfriends and I dressed up as Charlie's Angels so we had a sea of Kate Jacksons, Farrah Fawcetts and Jaclyn Smiths. The men showed up as sports stars: Bruce Jenner (pre-surgery), Mark Spitz and Kareem Abdul-Jabbar to name a few. We played Diana Ross, the Bee Gees and Led Zeppelin while eating ambrosia salad and cheesy dishes out of crockpots. We had two guests sleep on our lawn, but other than that, no issues.

Some party props.

During dinner Maddy says, "You lied to me." I have lied to the children many times so I stayed quiet to see what I was going to be accused of. "You said you NEVER did drugs." Everybody at the table was quiet as we waited for her to expound on her claim. "Remember the other night when I called you while I was watching *The Talented Mr. Ripley?*"

I did remember because I was out to dinner and she had called me multiple times in a panic: "Tom Ripley beat Dickie to death with an oar!" then "He's a serial killer! He murdered Freddie and Peter!" and "This movie is freaking me out!" At the time, I thought her reaction to the film was quite strong, but she's the middle child and melodramatic.

Maddy continued her story. "You have weed lollipops in your drawer," she accused me. I looked at my husband, who had coughed on his chicken, possibly because it was very, very dry but also because he was caught off guard. I, however, had no idea what anyone was talking about and gave everyone the confused puppy look.

Confused puppy look.

"I have never done drugs. That's the truth. What are you talking about?" I asked.

"You're hiding weed lollipops in your drawer and I KNOW they are weed, Mom, because I ate one and I felt really, really loopy."

It was true that I was a habitual hider of caramel, Twizzlers and sometimes taffy (but mostly chocolate items) in my drawers because we have so many kids that anything with sugar disappears in twenty seconds. I had recently switched to hiding my candy stash in the produce drawer because no children ever check under the kale. I knew there was still some candy in my drawer because I had thrown a bunch of lollipops in there that I had taken from the bank to use as decoys, but they weren't weed for God's sake.

Peter finally filled me in. "One of the guests from the party left you two special suckers. I hid them in your bedside drawer." I immediately knew who he was referring to: one of the funniest, nicest women on the planet who recently, had traveled to a weed legal state. She's super generous and must have shared her stash with us as a party gift.

As I ran to my bedroom, I screamed at Maddy, "How dare you go through my drawers!"

I ate the other weed lollipop while soaking in the tub watching *The Talented Mr. Ripley* on my iPad. Tom Ripley clubbing a swimsuit-clad Dickie with an oar did seem to come to life under my mild cannabis high.

Georgia voted "no" to the legalization of marijuana, which really stinks. Certainly, with all my conditions—being forty-five, trying to break into Hollywood, managing a family and a high-maintenance dog, all while trying to please the Lord—I would qualify as one who suffers and would gain access to all things 420. Dang Baptists.

THE ONLY SON

PJ was born with a rare x-linked recessive disease that many children do not survive. At any given time, only a handful of people in the world are born with WAS; he was misdiagnosed for over a year. It looks like eczema, a common rash children get, but PJ also had extremely low white-blood-cell counts that required him to live at Duke University for close to a year to get blood transfusions. Finally, after a year of being misdiagnosed, a DNA evaluation revealed the issue, Wiskott–Aldrich syndrome,[33] better known as WAS.

The only cure for WAS is a bone-marrow transplant and no one in the family was a match. When it was suggested that Peter reach out to his birth family (Peter had been adopted as a baby) for a matching donor, Peter agreed. His birth parents were not a match, but it opened the door to two new families. It's remarkable how, in the darkest of times, light is sometimes revealed.

The bone-marrow match ended up being PJ's sister, Savannah, who was five at the time. No one had thought of screening her but when she announced, "I'm going to save PJ," she was tested and was a perfect match. He's very fortunate to be so healthy, as most kids with WAS have lifelong health issues.

---

[33] To donate or learn more about WAS: www.wiskott.org/about-us/about-wiskott-aldrich-foundation

Savannah now uses her life-saving bone-marrow donation as leverage to get to eat the last piece of dessert or ride shotgun in the car. "Really PJ, you are taking the last piece? I SAVED YOUR LIFE." He normally acquiesces.

PJ had a period of arson and thievery when he was younger. He said he liked to "borrow" things from people's garages, but he never returned anything unless he got caught. When grounding him and making him do chores did not curtail the larceny, I decided to take him to jail.

A police officer met with us and told PJ about how the condemned live. "You never get to pick what you eat and you have to go to bed at the same time every night." This really didn't scare PJ because he currently had similar living conditions at our house. Only when the officer said the incarcerated took group showers and had no Internet access did PJ start to sweat. As the police officer walked us out he gave PJ his last words of warning: "Son, everybody hates a f****** thief."

The courthouse was within walking distance so we went and watched the judge sentence people for a couple hours. Witnessing police officers handcuffing and escorting kids—many just a few years older than himself—to jail curbed his sticky-fingers stage.

Don't write off your kids if they go through a rough patch. PJ is finishing up his final Eagle Scout requirements and works extremely hard in school. He has grown into a kind and generous kid, even though we do seem to have issues with common sense. During the Olympics, we were listening to the coverage of water polo. PJ asked with complete seriousness, "Water polo? How do they get the horses in the water?"

He also informed us, after a physician visited his school and spoke about the health risks of red meat, that he immediately wanted a diet with more "sea meats" and less "land meats."

HELEN

When Anna, my youngest daughter, and I were visiting Kristin in China we toured a facility that cared specifically for orphaned children that had heart issues. Kristin's sweet oldest daughter had selected the organization for her "Passion Project" for school.

The five children that lived in the orphanage were very well cared for by an equal number of employees. Each child had been given a more American/European-sounding name, in the hopes of making the child more appealing to adopt. Anna and I took turns holding Emily, Frank, Helen, Ashley and Walter while the director of the facility talked to us about the adoption process. "In China, you can only adopt a baby if you do not have any children of your own, but children with special needs are an exception." All five of the children were already in the process of being adopted by American families. Regardless, Anna wanted us to take either Helen or Walter with us.

I can't handle the four kids I'm already responsible for and assumed my husband would know that I was teasing him when I sent a picture of Anna holding a little girl with a text saying how great the facility was caring for the children with cardiac issues and finished with "Let's adopt a Helen!"

There's a twelve-hour time difference between Beijing and Atlanta so I didn't get an immediate reply. Kristin was hosting a cooking class at her house later that afternoon so we spent the day preparing for that. I was so busy I didn't check my phone until I was in bed for the night. I had a string of texts from Peter.

5:00 a.m. (Beijing Time)

Peter to me: How old is Helen?

5:01 a.m.

Will she need additional surgeries?

6:00 a.m.

Are you there? Ames? We're getting ready to put four through college, a new baby?

6:01 a.m.

I have been praying about why you were called to China and this must be it. You were meant to bring home Helen.

6:45 a.m.

We are fortunate to have the resources to help this child, we can do it.

Peter called me several times, but I was asleep. He left a message.

"Are you not getting my texts? Does Helen have a file that you can forward? I talked to all the kids and Savannah and Maddy are willing to share a room so you can bring Helen home. Call me!"

I finally checked my phone to find a stream of texts about all the plans he was making in preparation for Helen.

1:00 p.m.

Peter to me: We could modify the loft upstairs and make it into another bedroom and then adjoin the bathroom, if you hate that idea, the Clark's house just came on the market and it has a small bedroom on the main floor, but they have that sort of a brownish granite in the kitchen, we'd have to pull that out ... Call me.

2:00 p.m.

PJ thinks you are kidding about getting a Chinese baby, are you kidding? Text me ASAP.

3:00 p.m.

I'm at work and have made a few phone calls. There's a pediatric cardiologist in Atlanta! He needs details on Helen's situation.

"Oh my gosh! Peter thinks I really want a Chinese baby!" I read the string of texts to Kristin and she teared up because she thought it was so sweet that Peter was completely open to adopting a child based on one text from me saying *Let's adopt a Helen!*

"You have to get a Chinese baby now, Mom," Anna said.

Kristin looked at me and said, "Anna really wants a Chinese baby."

I asked Anna, "How about a cute Chinese dog instead of a baby?"

"Oh Mommy, that's a great idea! When can we get it?"

Kids are so fickle.

My husband, who had lost his first wife to cancer and almost lost a son to a very rare syndrome was still willing to take on a child with severe health issues and all the financial obligations that would accompany it. Peter is a very loving man and has forgiven me.

ATLANTA LAWN AND TENNIS ASSOCIATION (ALTA)

If you play tennis in Atlanta, you play in the Atlanta Lawn and Tennis Association (ALTA) League. It's lovely. Every Thursday the members of your team get decked out in adorable tennis outfits and visit swanky country clubs to play tennis and eat small, delicious sandwiches.

It was toward the end of the season and our team was neck and neck for points with our opponents, the ladies of a neighboring club.

Our opponents' tennis cabana sat on a steep incline, allowing for great views of their neighborhood and courts. The table was decorated with matching plates and napkins and a nice selection of sandwiches, salads and desserts. I was enjoying a ham, brie and apple sandwich with a side of homemade pasta salad when we heard *The Scuffle*.

We all lined the cabana to investigate the commotion. What had seemed like a strategy session of our opponents had turned into an outright fight. I'm not sure what they were saying because the ladies were speaking Japanese, but they became louder and more animated as the argument ensued.

We watched in bewilderment as one Asian woman started poking the other in the chest. The victim of the poking seemed to be taking the high road and headed for her bench. Seconds later, the player we thought was taking the high road grabbed the cooler and clocked her teammate in the face. We all raced down to what had developed into a wrestling match on the court. Below: not the actual cooler but one very similar.

Initially, the two captains tried to break up the battle, but it escalated to a 911 situation when there was bloodshed. The tiny, angry, Japanese ladies were still swinging at each other when they were cuffed and stuffed. We finished our gluten-free brownies and left.

They will have to sit the next tennis season out, as *All unsportsmanlike behavior will be reported to the League Office* is listed clearly in the ALTA rulebook.

HOT ITALIAN GUY #1
(NOT THAT INTO ME)

In college, I met a super-hot Italian guy named Rafello Hieronomo Graziano. Just kidding, his name was Brent, and we had French 101 together. In addition to being tall, dark and handsome, he was from Louisiana, could cook crawfish etouffee and had an adorable Creole/southern accent. All my friends loved him and he loved all my friends. The only person he seemed not to love was me.

Brent was in love with his ex-girlfriend, Lyndi. A clue that he was still in love with her would have been that he said on our first date, "I love girls with dark hair and blue eyes." Before I could even say thank you, he added, "My ex-girlfriend, Lyndi, had dark hair and blue eyes, too," and then showed me her picture that he kept in his wallet. I also knew about his lingering adoration because of all the evidence I uncovered while snooping through his stuff. I found notebooks of love letters to her, saying that he couldn't wait to "walk her down the aisle" and that their "children would go to the best schools."

I recognize that I was naive, spending a year with someone that so clearly was still in love with someone else. I'd argue that I'm optimistic. "He is so going to fall madly in love with me ... any minute now."

Eventually, I figured it out. One night at Brent's house, while getting some ice from the freezer, I heard grunting noises behind me. I turned to see Lyndi struggling to fit through the doggie door.

"What the F***?!"[34] I screamed.

Brent heard the ruckus, ran in and dropped to the floor to help her. "Lyndi, angel, why are you on the floor?" he asked while caressing her cheek and smoothing her *drunk and trying to squeeze through a doggie door* crazy hair. She smiled a big drunk smile and rested her head on his shoulder, still entangled in the door.

"Fine," I said, grabbing my purse from the counter. I wanted to make a dramatic exit but I had to open and close the door several times, all the while Lyndi's head was jolting back and forth. Finally, with both hands, I shoved her face and she fell backward, onto the garage floor.

I stepped over her and never looked back.

---

[34] My mother may disown me if I spelled out the actual expletives. For the record, I don't curse around my children, I curse at my children.

HOT ITALIAN GUY #2 (TOTALLY INTO ME, THEN NOT SO MUCH)

After pining for Brent to no avail for over a year, I was in a mood best described as *man-hating*, and my appearance reflected it. Why bother waxing your eyebrows and trying to be fit if you get nothing but heartbreak? I stopped coloring my hair so it was half-natural, half-not, like a poor woman's ombre.

To cheer me up, friends invited me to go skiing for the weekend, so we bundled up and headed to the exclusive ski slopes of Ohio. Everyone (except me) had their boyfriends with them, and one of the guys had brought a friend along, super-hot Italian Danny.[35]

Danny looked like he had jumped out of an Abercrombie & Fitch ad, which he sort of did because while working for A&F, an agent had spotted his chiseled face and offered him a contract to do local ads and stock photos. Imagine a showered and shaved Collin Ferrell that's more Italian and less Irish. That's what he looked like.

I was thick in my misanthropy period and did nothing but make snarky comments to Danny (when I wasn't just ignoring him) for the weekend. Turns out, he fell madly in love with me. All the

---

[35] Name changed

advice about looking your best and being sweet to get a man … could be false. Being caustic and slightly dirty[36] was working wonders for me.

For a while, Danny was the best boyfriend ever. He would take me to the ballet or foreign films and say things to me in Italian. In return, I would boss him around and complain about everything. His mother hated me. Even though she spoke very little English and I didn't know exactly what "Molto skinny Americano no Cattolico!"[37] meant, I knew it wasn't welcoming.

The longer Danny and I dated, the more I realized that he was an eleven on the looks chart and I was a six, maybe a seven with makeup and a push-up bra. At a party, a girl asked, "Who's the hottie?" My roommate answered, "Amy's boyfriend, Danny." Completely perplexed she screeched to me, "That guy dates you?"

Eventually, my faux confidence wore off and Danny and I were on the rocks—perhaps because I demanded that he spend every second with me and would incessantly badger him about what color the bridesmaids' dresses should be at our wedding, petal pink or plum purple.

As college graduation approached, things were stale. I begged my mother to take me to Italy as a graduation present because I wanted Danny to think that I was worldly and invested in learning about his homeland. Plus, being away from one another for a month may make his heart grow fonder.

My mom and I had a great visit to Rome, Venice, Florence and Milan. Having never escaped the tristate area, I bought Danny what I thought were great Italian gifts: pasta, a leather belt and

---

[36] Dirty in a disheveled way, not in a sexy or seductive way.
[37] "Very skinny American, not Catholic!"

a super-cool jacket from a boutique store. When I returned from Italy and gave him the pasta, he said, "You can buy this in the grocery store."

I moved on to the belt (too big) and the super-cool Italian jacket. "Try it on," I said.

His super beefy arms wouldn't squeeze into the sleeves. When he took it off, he held up the tag and said, "This is made in China."

Danny and I broke up less than a month after I returned from Italy, not because I gave him crappy gifts, but he gave me itchy crabs.[38] The whole time I was in Italy scouting our honeymoon spots and buying what I believed to be perfectly acceptable Italian treasures, he had been canoodling with a girl that worked at Victoria's Secret. *E' la vita* (that's life).

---

[38] It could have been a bubble-bath rash; regardless, it was over.

WHEN ALL ELSE FAILS
MAKE CHOCOLATE CHIP COOKIES

Cookies can really cheer a girl up. I'm a terrible baker but my friend, Lise Ode, provides a step-by-step video of how to make the best chocolate chip cookies on the planet, officially named: Chewy Chocolate Chip M&M Cookies.[39]

2 and 1/4 cups all-purpose flour
1 teaspoon baking soda
1 and 1/2 teaspoons cornstarch
3/4 teaspoon salt
3/4 cup (1.5 sticks) unsalted butter, melted
3/4 cup light brown sugar, loosely packed
1/2 cup granulated sugar[40]
1 large egg + 1 egg yolk (preferably at room temperature)
1 tablespoon vanilla extract
1 cup chocolate chips
1/2 cup M&Ms for tops of cookies

Preheat the oven to 350°F. Line two large baking sheets with parchment paper or silicone baking mats. Set aside.

Toss together flour, baking soda, cornstarch and salt in a large bowl. Set aside.

---

[39] Watch Lise's videos on Facebook and follow her blog Mom Loves Baking.
[40] Granulated sugar is probably the sugar you have in your pantry, like Domino brand. It will say granulated sugar on the packaging.

In a medium size bowl, whisk the melted butter, brown sugar, and white sugar together until no brown sugar lumps remain. Whisk in the egg, then the egg yolk. Finally, whisk in the vanilla.

Pour the wet ingredients into the dry ingredients and mix together with a large spoon or rubber spatula. The dough will be very soft, yet thick. Fold[41] in the chocolate chips. They may not stick to the dough because of the melted butter, but do your best to have them evenly dispersed among the dough.

Cover the dough and chill for 2 hours, or up to 3 days. Chilling is mandatory.[42]

Take the dough out of the refrigerator and allow to slightly soften at room temperature for 10 minutes.

Roll the dough into balls, about 3 tablespoons of dough each and place 2 inches apart on cookie sheets, or use a cookie scooper.

Bake the cookies for 11-14 minutes. They will look very soft and underbaked. They will continue to bake on the cookie sheet. Allow cooling on the cookie sheet for 10 minutes before moving to a wire rack[43] to cool completely.

Research shows that baking cookies reduces stress and boosts positivity. So ... cookies are good for you.

---

[41] To fold means gently combine a delicate mixture into a heavier mixture.
[42] If you're like me and have difficulty chilling both figuratively and literally, snack on the raw cookie dough during the refrigeration process. (Warning: eating raw eggs can cause salmonella poisoning.)
[43] I don't own any baking accessories so I let my cookies cool in the baking sheet, on a towel, on the counter.

121

MAKE BELIEVE LIFE

When I was in college, I worked as a nanny taking care of the children of wealthy couples living in swanky country club neighborhoods. It was a great gig. They paid me in cash, and I could wear whatever I wanted, eat their gourmet food and do my laundry in their super-load washers.

Coming from a small town, I was immensely enamored with their lives. They drove foreign cars, had expensive artwork and were always attending fabulous parties, charity events and traveling to exotic places.

My favorite clients had a giant house on the nicest golf course in Ohio. Their interior colors were limited to black, white and a touch of red. They had matching Mercedes-Benz sedans, closets filled with designer clothing and lots of staff. They employed housekeepers, landscapers, a swimming pool guy, a gentleman that had the garage code (allowing him access to detail their cars), plus both day and evening nannies.

The very glamorous mom of the house had been a clothing buyer for a large retailer and shared exciting stories about spotting the next trend at fashion shows in Paris and Milan. I believed that when I graduated from college I was going to be neighbors with her. I was wrong.

I DON'T LIKE REAL LIFE

When I graduated from college, it was 1993 and we were still typing our papers on word processors and going to a library to do research because the Internet didn't exist. Job opportunities were posted in the newspaper's Employment Section, and because newspapers charge by the line, the abbreviation for the job description was tough to decipher:

> *Admin. Clk req. type 40 wpm, cred ck, exc. writ skills. Own transp.*

This would be a common administrative-type job requiring typing, good credit and your own car. I would pay one dollar at the public library to fax my resume to various companies. Responses were slim. Most of the interviews went like this:

Hiring Manager: Give us an example of a time when you had to juggle multiple tasks under a deadline.

Me: Um … nothing is coming to mind.

Hiring Manager: Are you familiar with Microsoft Word, Excel and PowerPoint?

Me: No. No and no.

With a huge boyfriend breakup and no job prospects, I decided to try another market, so I packed my Honda Accord and moved south. In Atlanta, I headed to the Department of Housing and

Urban Development (because I wanted to help people) and asked for an application.

While I was filling out over 100 pages of paperwork, the recipients of HUD were coming in with angry complaints of no air-conditioning, broken appliances, smashed windows, missing checks in the mail, and dirty carpet, causing their child to have asthma.

These interactions filled me with passion. *I can help these people. They need help. They need homes. They ' re not being treated fairly*, I thought. I turned in my application and waited. Eventually, a HUD manager called me back.

HUD Manager: You forgot to check the boxes of the computer programs you know.

Me: I don't have any computer skills.

HUD Manager: The hundreds of other people that have applied do have computer skills. You can reapply if you gain any skills.

I applied to Delta Airlines to be a flight attendant and checked the box that said I could speak French to make myself look like I had an international flair. How much do flight attendants really say, anyway? *Des noisettes?* (Nuts?) *Boission?* (Drink?) I was sure I could pick up the rest when needed.

Unfortunately, I was interviewed by someone who was fluent in French. She rapidly fired questions at me and then scolded me for lying on the application: *"Tu ne parles pas français!"* (You do not speak French!)

"Apparemment pas assez, au revoir!" (Apparently not enough, goodbye!) I barked at her as I left.

Employment is a tricky game when people won't hire you unless you have experience, but how do you get experience if no one will hire you?

FALLING DOWN
LITERALLY AND FIGURATIVELY

Worst Fall

I finally landed my first real job out of college because a friend vouched for me and went to work for RTM in Atlanta. They owned over a thousand restaurants around the country and employed hundreds of accountants to manage their books. I was an assistant, supporting several regions.

My style idol in 1994 was Amanda Woodward, played by Heather Locklear from the hit show Melrose Place. Amanda was a no-holds-barred advertising executive that would lie, steal and cheat her way to the top, looking fabulous in her long jackets, short skirts, pantyhose and stilettos. I tried to dress exactly like her, even though I was an accounting assistant making nine dollars an hour.

Anyway, I was calculating many, many numbers in my Amanda Woodward–looking suit—long jacket, short skirt, thigh-highs, (because it's over 100 degrees in Atlanta in the summer and who can do payroll with a sweaty crotch?) and high heels—when I got a phone call requiring me to pick up a few reports downstairs. I had to walk to collect actual pieces of paper because the Internet had not been invented yet.

RTM had two very elaborate, winding sets of stairs that gracefully cascaded down to the beautiful marble floor of the lobby. They were very steep and had landings at the halfway points to break it up. The stairs were carpeted, presumably to make them less slippery. As I touched the first step, I was saying hello to one of my coworkers and my high heel caught on the carpet, propelling my body down the steps face-first. I gained so much momentum that I slid over the platform area, flailing and twisting as I tried to grab the handrail, and continued down the next flight.

I can still remember the fall: it was in slow motion, not unlike a car wreck. I was screaming obscenities in between grunts of pain and confusion. When I hit the bottom, I slid several feet on the marble floor of the lobby before coming to a stop at the feet of the group of visiting restaurant managers. I looked up to see twenty accountants gazing down from the glass balcony.

During the fall, my short skirt had rolled up to my hips, my thigh-high pantyhose had rolled down into sad, limp nets at my feet, and my underwear was showing—they read *Happy Buns* and featured a cheeseburger. As I tried to release my twisted left leg from under myself, I heard Jill, one of my bosses, ask, "Amy, are you alright?"

"Fine, I'm fine," I whimpered and hobbled out the front door to my car, only to realize I had left my purse and keys on the second floor. I cried for a while in the parking lot before hobbling back in to retrieve them.

Second-Worst Fall

When I was in my twenties, I was in Savannah with some girlfriends, and we attended Fleet Week, a United States Navy, Marine Corps and Coast Guard tradition in which active military ships recently deployed in overseas operations dock in a variety of major cities for one week.

Our Fleet Week was blessed with the United States Navy. Adorable, fit gentleman (and ladies) in their summer service whites descend to River Street by the thousands. As live bands play, the sailors are great sports, obliging tourists with sailor selfies[44] and enjoying the nightlife of Savannah.

Savannah is an old port and the streets are made of ballast stone. European ships, coming over to get Savannah's cotton, would arrive with their ships filled with stones to stabilize them. At port, they would dump all the rocks in the sea. The stones now line the streets and are very beautiful but they create a walking challenge if you're wearing any sort of heel and/or have had any adult beverages.

Everyone was dancing and having a great time when I decided to try to jump into my sailor's arms. I accidently kneed him in the groin and he dropped like a rock, onto the rocks, with me beneath him. After what seemed like several minutes, but was probably only a few seconds, he jumped up, grabbing my arm and jerking me off the ground. When someone does hundreds of pushups every day, they're very strong. He accidently injured my neck.

The pain was excruciating and my neck was stuck in a severe sideways pose. I looked like I suffered from some sort of palsy. I didn't want to disrupt anyone else's night so I slowly plodded to a bench and tried to look as natural as possible. People thought I was either straining to see something or doing some nighttime neck stretches.[45]

---

[44] These "selfies" were taken with cameras that required film and several days to process.

[45] www.universityorthopedics.com

Finally, my girlfriends schlepped me to the hotel and gave me some Tylenol PM and the remote. After three weeks, I could finally move my neck normally.

Worst Fall Not My Own

My friend Shannon is a yoga instructor. Saying someone's a yoga instructor exudes everything wonderful and positive in the world, which she is. My friend Beverly and I do not even gossip around her because she's so pure. When Shannon and I play tennis, I always tell our opponents she teaches yoga because they instantly know that the match is going to be honorable. Yoga teachers don't cheat online calls or throw out *Mother F*****!* if they miss a shot. She's literally balanced and can do the Eka Hasta Vrksasana (that's the one-handed tree pose for those of us that are not yogis) without even stretching.

Shannon was treating her two adorable girls and their friends to mani-pedis and Chipotle for lunch, surely celebrating good grades or accomplishments, things I personally am not that familiar with. The group ordered and found a table. When they called her number to pick up her black bean, peppers, onions, pico de gallo and extra guacamole salad bowl, her salon-issued disposable flop curled under her foot, evoking a cartoon-character-level slip and fall.

Black beans and guacamole exploded all over Shannon and several Russian businessmen that had come in after Shannon's group. A sixteen-year-old female employee told her flatly, "You can get another salad if you want," but no inquiry was made to her possible broken tailbone. Less than ten minutes later, she got up to refill her Coke and fell AGAIN with the same velocity as the first fall (damn you, flimsy flops!) as the Russians were still wiping the pico de gallo off their ties from the original fall.

Shannon sued Chipotle for $9 million[46] and moved to Maui where she hosts yoga retreats for women who want to cultivate discernment, awareness, self-regulation and a higher consciousness level.

---

[46] Shannon did not sue Chipotle; she's too nice.

FIFTY-FIVE HOURS A WEEK

For over ten years I worked for one of the largest employment agencies in the world. My Atlanta group had thousands of contractors, from file clerks to certified accountants, contracting for companies all over the city.

I loved being a recruiter. I got to help people land their first jobs or move people into better positions—and I got a commission. Plus, I always had great stories about all the crazy people I encountered in the world of temporary staffing.

Many of the applicants were educated professionals that were taking contract jobs to "get in the door" of large firms or had just moved and needed something immediately. However, most of the candidates were crazy and could not hold down a full-time job. About a third of the people that applied were unqualified due to their criminal background history, credit issues and/or drug usage.

One woman, working at a manufacturing facility, fell in love with the accounting supervisor and then discovered he was married. For weeks, she drove a van with a banner on the sides that read "Joe is a cheat."

We had multiple men apply for jobs and then show up for the contract as women. Neither we nor our clients cared if people were transgender or cross-dressers; they just needed to pick a gender and stick with it for that assignment.

We had a slew of daily cancellations, and contractors had lots of excuses for why they couldn't work. Sick children and car problems were the most common but we heard everything: doctor/dentist/orthodontist appointments, parent-teacher conferences, out-of-state visitors, quitting because they hate the job/manager/pay/location, interviewing for other jobs, and even "to get an abortion."

Mike, who was already on probation for missing so much work, called to tell us that that his mother-in-law was in a car wreck and had been beheaded. Our office called his employer (our client) and got him the week off. We sent flowers to his home. On Friday, when his wife came to pick up his paycheck, my entire staff greeted her with hugs and condolences for her mother's tragic passing. She had no idea what anyone was talking about and said the only reason she was picking up his check was that he was at a NASCAR race in Birmingham.

We would have to remove contractors from our client sites for every issue imaginable: sexual harassment, fighting on the job, stealing company materials, handing out religious or political information, accessing pornography, and lying on time cards. And these were the people that passed the background check.

Good help is really hard to find.

I GOT FIRED

THE FIRST TIME

I was fired from Burger King when I was in high school because I only wanted to run the drive-thru. I loved wearing the headset and calling in orders.

When the manager approached me with what looked like a large putty knife and told me to scrape the gum off the underside of the tables, I insisted, "But I'm the drive-thru girl!"

He handed me the spackle knife and said, "Scrape." I turned in my blue polyester shirt and BK visor and left.

THE SECOND TIME I GOT FIRED

When I worked for a jewelry store at Christmastime, I accidently forgot to take a customer's engagement ring out of the ultrasonic jewelry cleaning machine. On Christmas morning, his fiancée opened a neatly wrapped, yet empty box. My boss told me that he really didn't need any more holiday help.

THE THIRD TIME I WAS FIRED

I was fired from a call-center job in college because I found out the charity I was collecting for was bogus so I spent my time calling as many people as I could and told them as much. My sales were zero for the week.

I WAS FIRED TWICE IN ONE SUMMER

I loved working at the Cinema and Draft House in Atlanta. I was a waitress for the movie complex/restaurant and worked with twenty other college students. When the manager invited me to go to a concert, I thought it was a company event and said yes. (I was eighteen.)

When he picked me up, it was just him—he thought it was a date, complete with strawberries and champagne. Awkwardly, I pecked him on the cheek when he dropped me off after the concert.

On my next shift, a fellow waitress asked me about my weekend. I told her how embarrassed I was, thinking it was a company event but the manager thought it was a date. She paused for a second and then said, "He's my husband." When I went to check the schedule, my name was crossed off.

The same summer I worked another great job, driving a beverage cart at a swanky Country Club. The club had a great little library, stocked with classic books, so in between course loops or while waiting for someone to play through, I could read.

That job ended when I cut across the green at exactly the wrong time, taking a golf ball to my head and denying Mr. Lupinbocker what he swore would have been a hole-in-one. The club was more concerned with my interruption of Mr. Lupinbocker's shot than the goose egg developing near my brain. I could've been suffering an intracerebral hematoma, as I was experiencing a lot of dizziness, nonetheless, I was informed that the summer position had ended.

ALMOST FIRED

When I managed a staffing firm, we had to collect two forms of identification from every potential employee. The most common documents provided were driver's licenses and Social Security cards. The copier was in the break room and my employees and I had an ongoing contest of finding the worst driver's license photos and then taping them on the wall. An employee reported us to our regional manager who read us the riot act ... but I saw her smiling as she took them down.

FIRED FROM BABYSITTING JOB

I worked for about a year for a woman in Dublin, Ohio, that had four small children. Her kids were good, but there were four of them and they required constant nose and bottom wiping, snacks and refilling sippy cups, cleaning up messes and breaking up scrabbles. The mom told me proudly, as she was headed out the door to run errands, "We're having another baby!"

Her husband worked at least seventy hours a week, traveled extensively and was taking Paxil and several other prescriptions that were labeled "Not to be taken by mouth, insert into rectum." (I stumbled across them while looking for the maraschino cherries for my giant bowl of ice cream I consumed once I put the kids to bed.)

My face must have curled up into a look of disdain/disgust/confusion as I asked, "Why?"

"We love children!" she snapped at me.

Even though I tried to backpedal with, "That's wonderful!" she must have felt my contempt. I was never invited back.

WAS NEVER HIRED

When I graduated from college, I applied to work at a local paper in Columbus, Ohio. A very attractive gentleman sat me in his office but was interrupted by a coworker. He excused himself, telling me to make myself comfortable.

While he was out, I reapplied my lipstick and noticed a tiny scab on my temple, which I couldn't resist scraping off. I'm a popper/squeezer and will operate on any foreign bumps or lumps that I can reach on my body.

When he returned, his demeanor had totally changed. He asked me, "Are you alright?"

I looked down to see drops of blood all over my resume. In a panic, I flung the bloody papers and started wiping my face with my hands.

It's tough to interview when you're hemorrhaging and saying sorry a thousand times.

I was not called back for a second interview.

FIGHTING THE MAN GOT ME FIRED

Within the staffing industry, I was promoted to a corporate role of training and development. It was the best job in the world. My coworker and I got to travel around the U.S. conducting sales and new-hire training. The only downside was the firm we worked for had a reputation of being "big and cheap."

The national-accounts division would offer clients huge discounts if they gave us an exclusive, which eroded our margins—more work, less commission. When the economy was doing well, they started acquiring boutique firms, which had amazing margins because they gave their contractors fantastic

136

benefits and placed them at the best companies in the market. They treated their clients to all sorts of appreciation parties and vacations. If you have the best candidates, you can place them in the best companies and vice versa. It creates a wonderful, positive cycle or what is known in the industry as "referrals and residuals."

Unfortunately, once the super-big-and-cheap staffing firm acquired the boutique firms, they immediately shoved rules and regulations down their throats. Corporate would strip the boutiques of their great benefits, force them to staff the large, low-margin accounts and then wonder why, within six months, their newly acquired gems had tremendous turnover of management and recruiters, lost their best contractors and started having crappy margins, just like their other 1,000 offices.

When the company took a recently acquired IT firm and made them move into cubicles from their cool office with basketball hoops and pinball tables and stripped them of all their benefits, people started to complain. Since the head of human resources (everyone called him The Rat because he was notorious for trying to cheat employees, and coincidentally, he had a rat-like face) happened to be in the Atlanta office, I questioned him.

Rat: I don't like your tone. I'm the head of HR and have visibility into situations that *you* would never understand.

Me: You bought XYZ firm for their high margins?

Rat: Acquisitions are very complex, but yes, that is always a factor.

Me: But you made them move from their cool office space, will not allow them to take their top clients on trips and stripped the contractors of all their benefits?

Rat: They will have the same benefits we all have here at *We are super-big-and-cheap staffing firm.*[47]

Me: And you never wonder why everyone quits and the margins fall to s*** within six months?

Rat: Who. Is. Your. Boss?

At the time, I was a single mom.

---

[47] Benefits at Super-Big-and-Cheap staffing firm were total dog s***.

I AM AN ACTRESS

I auditioned to land a recurring role at the mega church I attend in Atlanta. When I completed my audition, they gave me the "We'll call you, don't call us" answer. Two weeks went by with still no news, so I followed up with a phone call. I got, "We are still auditioning," followed by, "If we are interested, we'll let you know." About a month later I did get a call: "When can you start?"

I found out that they were TRYING to get people to audition and no one showed up, so I got the part by default. The role of the "Host" is to warm up the audience with games before the more serious Bible Storyteller comes out. Forty Sundays a year, I get to go on stage in front of 200-300 second and third graders and get them fired up for Jesus. It's my favorite part of the week.

Although we are all volunteers and Christians, we are also actors and what we want most is to be center stage. The more the ridiculous the costumes, the better the skit. Last month the Bible Story called for the Host to be "Grapes." The grape suit is hilarious, purple and wiggly.

The Bible Storyteller informed me, the morning of the show, that she had selected one of the worship singers to be the "Grapes," and that I could lead the children on stage as we acted out the Moses-sending-spies story.

"Why am I not the Grapes?" I asked.

She replied, "It doesn't matter who's the grapes."

When I finished rehearsal, I walked out to get a bottle of water and ran into Stephen, the "Host" for the earlier service. "Hey, Grapes," he said. I asked if he got to be the Grapes at the nine o'clock service and he said, "Of course!"

I saw the director out of the corner of my eye and took the case to her.

"May I please be the Grapes?"

The director went into my room and told the production manager, "Amy is the Grapes," and then left.

"You took this to management?" the Bible Storyteller asked.

"Yes," I replied. "I am the Grapes."[48]

---

[48] Why are grapes in the Bible? Grapes are referenced in the story of Moses asking a group of men to act like spies to check out the area of Canaan. The spies found everything to be giant. *When they came to the valley of Eshcol, they cut down a branch with a single cluster of grapes so large that it took two of them to carry it on a pole between them! Numbers 13:23.* The spies betrayed God by lying about the area, so he made them wonder around the wilderness for forty years. See BIBLE.

THINGS THAT AGGRAVATE ME

1. Horror movies. Why in the world would I want to be scared to death in a dark room with strangers?

2. Annoying noises. People that chomp, slurp, tap their fingernails or hit the end of a pen seven hundred times drive me crazy. Misophonia is a newly recognized condition defined as *the dislike of sound that worsens over time and causes a combination of rage, panic, fear, terror and anger when triggered*, and I have it. As of today, there is *no effective treatment*. I self-medicate by telling people, "Stop that right now or I may kill you—I have a condition." That seems to be working.

3. People that call waiters by their names. It doesn't rattle me as much if you are asking the server's opinion, such as, "Karen, do you like the lobster bisque?" But when people complain using the waiter's name, it sounds like a personal attack. "Uhhh, Jenny! Hey, Jenny, this eggplant parmesan is cold as ice in the middle."

4. Smoking. I'm a libertarian so I don't care if you want to spend your money on something that poisons your body and makes your breath stink. My issues are when smokers throw their cigarettes out the window or dump their ashtrays in parking lots. Kill yourself slowly but don't f****** litter.

5. Dragging one's feet. What type of ambition, goals or dreams can you have if you can't even muster the energy to pick up your own feet?

6. Reply all. No one needs to know why you can't attend the baby shower/dinner party. If you must share that you are getting a root canal, reply ONLY to the originator of the email.

7. People whose babies are crying in public places and do nothing about it. One time I actually said to the parents "Hey, your baby is crying. Maybe you could pick them up."

8. Reality shows—because they do not employ WRITERS.

9. People that stop one inch from your bumper at a stop sign. Studies show that Americans prefer a social distance of 4 feet or more,[49] so I would prefer that the complete stranger in the 5,000 pound Silverado 3500 not ride my ass.

10. My children, when they still try to order crab legs in a restaurant as if it's their wedding anniversary although they have heard 1000 times "When you pay for your own meal, you can order whatever you want, but for now you're getting the chicken fingers from the kid's menu."

---

[49] www.//blogs.transparent.com/english/personal-space-an-american-perspective

ONE SAD STORY

Traci and Caroline

I had an older sister, Traci. Even though we looked almost identical, we were complete opposites. Her lifelong dream was to be married and have a lot of children. She wasn't interested in a career or material things, avoided the spotlight, rarely drank alcohol, and volunteered in her kids' schools, at church and at a Hope Crisis Center that helped new moms. I ... well, I already admitted we were opposites.

In August of 2013, Traci and her youngest daughter, Caroline, who was eleven, had spent the morning decorating Caroline's locker in preparation for her first year of middle school. After they finished putting chandeliers and Justin Bieber wallpaper in Caroline's locker, they were headed to the bowling alley to meet a group of friends and had just reached the car when it started to downpour.

Within three blocks of the middle school, Traci hydroplaned, ran into oncoming traffic and was killed instantly. Caroline spent three days in the ICU before the state of Georgia declared her brain-dead and turned off life support. Seven of her organs were used to save other children's lives, including her heart, which was implanted into a young girl in Georgia.

I wasn't worried about my sister's soul, as she was a devout Christian woman, but I was obsessed with her last moments of life. Did she know she was going to die? Did she think she was going to kill all the other passengers in the other car that she hit?[50] Did Caroline witness her own mother's death? I would go to sleep praying that she had not suffered and wake up only to start obsessing again. I could not move past— "Did she suffer?"

A few months after the accident, while attending a book club at my friend Rachel's house, I was reintroduced to Rachel's younger sister, Cristy. Rachel had told me many times that her sister was clairvoyant: Christy would wake up in the middle of the night from having a vision regarding a family member. Once she saw her grandfather, who had escaped from an assisted-living home and was wearing a striped shirt, trying to get into a closed Walmart.[51]

Cristy had recently moved into our neighborhood and joined our book club. She told me, "Your sister has been pestering me." I said nothing as we moved from the kitchen into the dining room. She continued, "Your sister. She has been pestering me to tell you some things. Would it be alright if I told you?" I nodded.

"Your sister wanted me to tell you that she loves you and that she has always loved you and that she is happy." I stared at her, not knowing what to say. "She also said that Caroline wanted

---

[50] The passengers she collided into suffered broken bones but thankfully survived.
[51] Cristy's father picked grandpa up exactly where she said he would be, outside Walmart, wearing a striped shirt.

Anna (my daughter) to have her sock-puppet animal." I told her I would look for it in Caroline's things. She hugged me for a long time and we started to head back to the kitchen. "Oh," she said, "and she wanted me to tell you that she saw a lot of trees and then it was over."

I have never had another experience like this in my life and I'm not sure what to make of it. I absolutely believe Cristy. I'm glad she told me, but I would have thought it would have been more comforting than it was.

This is a book of failures, so I will share where I failed my sister. Beginning in her forties, Traci suffered from MS. There were times when she couldn't sign her name because her hands felt as if they were asleep and were so tingly they hurt. Her ex-husband was on a rampage to get custody of their youngest daughter and had exhausted my sister emotionally and our family financially. Traci's middle daughter had run off to California to get married two days after graduating from high school and had returned divorced and expecting a new baby. My sister had so much stress and needed me, but I was so caught up in my own life, I wasn't there for her the way I should have been.

I also failed her horribly at the funeral. I walked up the steps of the stage, straightened out my notes on the podium and looked up to see the faces of little girls—Caroline's friends from school, gymnastics, soccer and church. They sat next to their mothers, all of them wiping their tears. My heart was so broken. Inside, I was screaming, *Why? How could this happen to my family? Look at my parents' faces. God, look at these little girls—look what you have done to them.* For some reason, standing there behind the podium, I didn't shed a tear. I started babbling about how my sister and I would fight as kids, trying to be funny, as if I could lighten the mood of a funeral. It was a disaster. Thank goodness, my sister's grown girls gave eloquent, appropriate speeches.

As I replay that morning in my head, I wish I would have said that I admired the way she kept her faith and sense of humor even in her darkest moments. A year before she died, Traci and her new husband had been thrown in jail for a ridiculous situation that was no fault of hers or her husband's. The police lied to them and our family, saying they were just going to ask them a few questions and release them. Instead, they retained them for four days—holding them over a holiday weekend.

Traci knew she was innocent and that this too would pass. After the trying weekend, she was released from jail and exonerated of all charges.

Within minutes of being sprung, she was hilariously recounting the trials and tribulations of spending the weekend in the county jail. She would re-enact the very poor room service being provided in the clink. "Excuse me, excuse me, sir, may I get a little blanket?" She would make a grouchy guard face and scream "NO!"

She would say nicely, "I'm sorry for asking. I was just a little cold, there's no blanket and it looks as if I'm sleeping over ..."

I must have asked her to tell the jail story a hundred times because it was so funny the way she imitated the guards and the other inmates. But looking back, it's something bigger to me now. It was my big sister showing me that humor and grace can carry you through life's biggest shit sandwiches.

I think she would love that I'm sharing a tiny piece of her story.

STEPMOMMYING IS SUPER F******* TOUGH

Together, we have four kids: Savannah, Maddison, PJ and Anna. They're all teenagers, and this was our Christmas card a few years ago.

I tried to get a different pose, thirty seconds after the first, but Maddy slapped Anna because she wanted to sit in the front.

Even if you have the best kids in the whole world, they are still very difficult to live with. They lie a lot and are not concerned about personal hygiene or tidiness. We're trying to raise kind, responsible adults that will move out one day and get jobs. We give them a few, reasonable chores so they won't grow up to be entitled a**holes.

In line with this, the kids are supposed to change their sheets every Friday. Sometimes they take their sheets off and throw them into the washer but invariably forget to put them in the dryer and the three other kids aren't going to move their sibling's sheets from the washer to the dryer so the laundry is overflowing and at night no one has sheets. They sleep on bare mattresses, sometimes for days.

Me: Put sheets on your beds.

Kids: Why?

Me: You wash and dry the sheets, then put them back on your bed before you sleep. That's the process.

Kids: Why?

Me: It's unhygienic to sleep on a bed without sheets.

Kids: Why do you care? You're not sleeping in my bed.

Me: Because we do not live in a crack house, that's why.

The kids are not allowed to eat food in their rooms and compliance is about 80 percent. Maddy is the worst on this issue. At any given moment, we find ten or more mugs of congealed chocolate milk under her bed. I finally removed the bed frame so now she hides them in her attic space. Once I found a bowl of shrimp bisque under her bathroom counter and ham sandwich remnants in her desk drawer.

When I complained to my friend Jen, "I found a ham sandwich in a desk drawer," she asked with sincerity, "Oh no, does she have an eating disorder?"

"No, slob," I replied.

So far, our grossest incident when we banished PJ, then ten, to the car for a few minutes while the rest of the family ran into the Verizon Store. PJ had to stay in the car because he had told a sister to "shut up" a few minutes earlier. The air conditioner was on and we were all of twenty yards away so he was never in any danger. The last words my husband uttered were, "Do not leave this car for ANY reason."

We finished getting a charger and piled back into the car and into the most horrific stench. "OH MY GOSH! IT SMELLS LIKE DOG POOP IN HERE!" the older one screeched.

PJ then handed Peter a Target bag that was still warm—because of the poop it contained. "You told me not to leave the car for ANY reason," he smirked. I'm sure everything will work out with our children, we are just going through a rough patch.[52]

---

[52] Some days we drink more than others.

HAIR PROBLEMS

In the 1980s our role models were Cyndi Lauper and Madonna. It was the era of John Hughes' movies, *Breakfast Club* and *Pretty in Pink*. Regardless of whether you were a "preppy," "stoner," "jock," or "nerd," your hair goals were the same—huge. Because our products were limited in the 1980s, our volume came from spiral perms, a teasing comb and Aqua Net.

In high school, I went to the local beauty school for perms because it was cheaper than the salon. (You could get all-over highlights for around fifteen dollars.) The "beauty student" suggested I get a perm and then highlights because my hair was "limp and lifeless." The combination of perm solution, hydrogen peroxide and ammonia broke my hair off just below my ears, propelling the new curls to almost gravity-defying heights, so she slathered it with oil. I resembled one of the Jackson Five, and not in a good way.

Our 1989 Marietta Senior High School graduation hair.[53]

Me   Susan

---

[53] I thought my hair was so fabulous in college that I applied to be a model and paid over $500 for headshots. Return on investment: zero.

Kristin   Marilyn

My hair has been many colors: green from years of pool chlorine, orange from excessive use of Sun-In Hair Lightener, and pink-to-dark-purple as I experimented with reds. *Hair color may vary,* the box warns you.

My worst hair event came when I had just started dating husband number two and my stylist had an emergency, so she gave her clients to her partner, a super-nice guy that didn't speak any English. I believe he was Korean. I held up my pointer finger and thumb, demonstrating *an inch,* and instructed him to "Just take off an inch all over, a trim." He confirmed, showing one inch with his fingers. He then grabbed the top section of my hair and cut it down to an inch.

There are many women that can rock a super, super-short haircut. Regrettably, I am not one of them.

WHAT'S WRONG WITH THE DOG?

When I married Peter, I inherited three kids and one dog, Cooper Sapelo. To Peter's chagrin, I transitioned Cooper from an outdoor dog to an indoor dog.

"You have changed my hunting dog into a Yorkie," he complained, even though Cooper adjusted well to being fed the kids' vegetables under the dinner table and sleeping at my feet.

Recently his fur started falling out. We had him examined for fleas, ticks and mites—things that make dogs itchy and subsequently may make their fur come off in patches—but Cooper was clear of all critters. Our vet said sometimes an animal's fur falls out because it has anxiety. Cooper doesn't have a lot of anxiety; after all, his days are filled with fun and relaxation ...

Going on walks ...

Chasing tennis balls and eating snacks with his friends ...

Taco Buffa

Hazel Shires

Brody and Sugar Ryals

Henry Summerville

Having sleepover parties with his girlfriend, Molly Carter...

Hanging out with his best friends, Floyd Delp and Truffles Krogman ...

and eating ice cream and going swimming.

Even with all of this, given the vet's comments regarding anxiety, I googled "dog trauma/anxiety" and found that Cooper did exhibit some of the traits associated with dog anxiety: excessive itching and licking, sometimes pooping on the floor, and seeming slightly insecure (never wanting to leave my side). But he didn't demonstrate any other signs: shaking, howling or barking, or coprophagia (thank goodness—that's the condition where dogs eat their own waste). Cooper loved to eat horse waste, guinea pig waste, cat waste and goose waste but so far had stayed clear of his own feces. He also didn't hide from us or run away, yet his fur kept falling out, which started to give me anxiety.

From my online research, I got a list of anxiety-reducing actions that could help Cooper relax: playing soft music, cuddling, rubbing him with essential oils, and making sure he had lots of exercise. We followed a strict regimen of cuddling, walking, and playing only soothing Norah Jones tunes, but he was getting more and more bald spots.

I ordered and started administering VetriScience Composure Behavior Health Bite-Sized Dog Chews. They're supposed to "improve your dog's cognitive function without changing your dog's personality." You could double or triple the dosage if you did not see improvements. Within a week, I was going through bags of the chews, which Cooper really enjoyed, but which did not reduce his excessive itching or his fur dropping out in clumps … and they gave him stinky farts.

Veterinarian David did blood tests and everything came out great. We changed Cooper's food and had him wear a cone around his neck, which really confused him. He would walk into walls and then just stand, staring at the wall, wagging his tail.

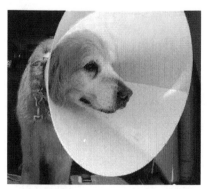

Cooper wearing the cone of shame

We were baffled. Our next step was cognitive behavioral therapy—a doggie shrink. What other options did we have? His coat looked dry and he started scratching the bare spots bloody.

The mystery of Cooper's fur was solved on a Thursday. I was on my way to tennis when I realized I had forgotten my food assignment and needed to return to the house. I ran in the side door to see the housekeeper spraying Cooper with a can of Febreze.

"Juan, noooooooooo. You cannot spray Cooper with Febreze," I said as calmly as I could. Juan looked confused and kept spraying.

"NO SPRAY PERRO!" I insisted.

Juan said, "Hedores!" (stinks/smells), which was accurate. I stared Juan down and took the can.

"Haciéndole enferma,"[54] (making him ill) I said sadly, pointing to Cooper's diminishing coat.

"OKAY! NO SPRAY!" he agreed.

Within a few months, Cooper's shagginess level was back to normal. However, he had grown accustomed to the VetriScience Composure Behavior Health Bite-Sized Dog Chews, soft music and essential oils. And who are we to deny him? We take turns giving him doggie massages.

---

[54] I don't speak any Spanish whatsoever and communicated everything via wild hand gestures.

THE WRONG MESSAGE

Our girls grew up obsessed with the tales of princesses in books, movies and television. We had every type of princess product imaginable: coloring books, Barbie princesses, gowns, shoes, shirts, pajamas, lunchboxes, wands, tiaras, clip-on earrings, posters, hair brushes, night-lights and bedspreads. I like the princess message of kindness and grace, but I did not like the theme "Be kind and generous and you too will be able to land a man."

I think the message of how to land a man was confusing to little girls. Both Sleeping Beauty and Snow White were cursed by older, jealous hags. Sleeping Beauty falls into a forever sleep and Snow White is thought to be dead. The sleeping/dead princesses are laid out to be mourned by their families or dwarfs. Eventually, princes come by, fall instantly in love with them, and with one kiss, they awake and start to plan their weddings.

Sleeping Beauty and Snow White married people they had never met. Belle was willing to marry a hot-tempered bigfoot-type creature. And poor Ariel! She made the ultimate sacrifice to win her man, leaving her home and family forever and changing into another species.

Today the princess movies are about the princess finding herself, rather than a man. More women than ever before are CEOs, physicians, attorneys and senators and that feels like progress. As women, have we moved on from ranking our self-worth by "getting a man"?

Apparently, it is still an issue:

how to get a man

About 928,000,000 results (0.75 seconds)
That's almost a billion results. Ladies, we need to keep working on this.

All the single ladies, marriage can be good, but it is not all roses and love. Ask your married friends, with kids, what they spend most of their time doing and their answers will be along the lines of "Arguing about how to discipline the children in-between doing immense amounts of laundry."

IT'S YOUR VAJAYJAY

I was in the dressing room at the mall and complimented a woman, Regina,[55] on her outfit. She proceeded to tell me how she had once weighed over four hundred pounds. A small crowd gathered around us as she continued.

Three years ago, she had called the credit card company, inquiring a charge for "Paddles" in New York City. She discovered that her husband, Frank, had invited Marti, her best friend, on a business trip. Together they charged $1,200 at a bondage, discipline, dominance and submission, sadomasochism (BDSM) sex club. Basically, they were paying to drink ticky-tacky cocktails and get spanked on West 26th.

Regina, after researching divorce law, learned that marital debt is split between both parties, so she promptly maxed out every credit card to pay for a face-lift, breast augmentation, hair extensions, vaginal rejuvenation, and gastric bypass surgery before filing for divorce. She had lost close to 200 pounds and was treating herself to a new wardrobe. Other women started commenting on everything from their divorce disasters to weight struggles and how they too had overcome even the worst of what life handed them.

My point is that women love to share and we all benefit from it. Most of my girlfriends are my age so we chat about our

---

[55] Not her real name.

husbands, jobs, kids, and lately, the bevy of tests required for ladies our age. We need colonoscopies, mammograms, and pap smears, as well as our cholesterol checked. When having your breasts squeezed or cold instruments inserted into your vagina, referrals are critical.

While enjoying lunch at our favorite Thai place, Sharon, Melissa, and I started talking OB/GYN appointments.

Sharon: Dr. B[56] is great, so personable. Sometimes we talk for ten to fifteen minutes.

Melissa: Are you naked or dressed during these conversations?

Sharon: It could be before, after or during the exam.

Me: He's eyeball to eyeball with your vagina and you're chatting for fifteen minutes?

Sharon: Yes. He asks how often I work out because my abdominal muscles are tight and we talk about our passion for working out.

Me: That's unprofessional loitering on your vajayjay He's just distracting you so he can spend more time inside your body. That's inappropriate. You should report him.

Sharon sets her fork down and says firmly: He's nice and makes me feel good about my body.

Me: Melissa, are you listening to this? Please tell Sharon she's getting sexually exploited by her doctor and should report him immediately.

Melissa: Amy, shush! Sharon, can I get his card?

---

[56] Doctor B has recently retired.

MY MOTHER

I am very proud of my mother and adore her, however ...

1. She confuses real-life news with television shows. "There's a kidnapper wearing a bunny-rabbit mask on the loose." "That's CSI, Mom." (season two, episode 14) "Well, it's still really scary."

2. Kate Middleton is her benchmark. "Do you think Kate Middleton would use such language, Amy? Be a lady."

3. She's a mini-hoarder. "Do you want seven pounds of cookies? I just wanted the Thomas Kinkade tins."

4. She believes women should serve their men. I was holding a baby—while vacuuming—when she suggested, "You should fix your hair a little bit and get your husband a glass of tea," while he was on the riding lawn mower.

5. She likes to gamble. "I got the triple, triple, double, double, seven and won two hundred dollars!"

6. One event during the week can throw her entire schedule off. "No, I cannot go to lunch on Tuesday, Amy. I'm renewing my license on Thursday and need to get ready."

7. She would do anything for almost anyone. Ten years ago, she GAVE A KIDNEY to a coworker.

8. She drives 45 mph in the fast lane but yells at the people honking at her, "I pay my taxes! This is my lane too!"

9. She will schedule, and will not reschedule, a whole day around mopping her floors.

10. She doesn't go to the doctor. No mammograms or colonoscopies for my mom. *If God wants me, he can have me,* is her motto.

11. We are very close. I call her every day. If I didn't call her, we would never speak again as she *does not call people* and *cannot figure out the smartphone.*

Ahh, moms are funny.

WHAT'S WRONG WITH THE BAND?

Peter graduated from Georgia Tech, which is consistently ranked as one of the top ten (public) schools in the country. He was really good in math and science and won a science contest that landed him an internship at the CDC when he was a junior in high school. He was recruited by the Air Force and Naval Academies, Stanford, and other swanky places that only admit about 2 percent of the people that apply. He picked GA Tech.

I went to The Ohio State University in Columbus, Ohio, which is a fine school. We are most proud of alums John Kasich (presidential candidate), Jack Nicklaus (golfer) and Les Wexner (founder of The Limited Corporation). We also can claim George Steinbrenner, Charles Kettering, and Dwight Yoakam, per Wikipedia, as "attended." Regrettably, deplorable serial killer/cannibal Jeffrey Dahmer also briefly attended my alma mater. We don't list him in any of our marketing materials.

Georgia Tech claims Jeff Foxworthy as "attending." Graduates include former President Jimmy Carter; Admiral James A. Winnefeld, former Joint Chiefs-of-Staff; John Brock, CEO of Coca-Cola; two Nobel Peace Prize recipients; and fourteen astronauts.

Recently we went to the Georgia Tech homecoming game. At halftime, I was excited for their band performance. I grew up with an award-winning high school band and my beloved Ohio

State always ranks in the top bands in the country.[57] The Associated Press reported Ohio State's band is known for its "spectacularly complex performances." The Michael Jackson halftime tribute show from 2013 has been viewed more than 11.6 million times as the entire band formed a moving "moonwalk" while playing "Beat It" and "Billie Jean."

Ohio State marching band's moonwalk.[58]

Even in the 1940s the Buckeyes cried out the "We Don't Give a Damn" for the whole State of Michigan song.

So, at halftime at the GT homecoming, when the announcer said, "This next song is dedicated to the field of math," and then expounded on why math is so important, mentioning, "cartesian coordinates" and "fermat primes," I got a little lost. I majored in human ecology to avoid taking calculus.

Lyrics to the Georgia Tech Differential "X" Song

> *Differential "X" !*
>
> *Differential "Y" !*
>
> *"A" square, "B" square*

---

[57] www.Ranking of College bands
[58] www.youtube.com/watch?v=GTca2nrln4U OSU band moon walk video.

Integral of pi!

Another version of the song:

E to the X dy dx,

E to the X dx,
Tangent Secant Cosine Sine,
3.14159,
Square roots, cube roots, Poisson brackets,
Disintegrate ' em Yellow Jackets!

They are REALLY into mathematics. Very few students attended the homecoming game, probably because they were studying as they must take multivariable calculus and something called discrete mathematics. The Duke University students' section (Tech's homecoming game opponents) were louder than the entire stadium of Tech students and fans. Are football games too old-school?

We sat with a group of Peter's Sigma Nu fraternity brothers and other people that had graduated over twenty-five years ago. They still had some fire in them, yelling, "Do you not even want to win, Paul Johnson?" to the Tech coach. A gentleman in front of us was screaming the names of the Tech players AND the Duke players. At one point when Tech was behind, he yelled to the Duke quarterback, "Thomas Sirk, you can burn in hell!" Tech won 38-35.

After, we went to the Sigma Nu house where they were offering "Shitty Beer" for two dollars and "Good Beer" for three dollars. Peter's fraternity brothers sat around the pool, reminiscing about who had been maimed by jumping off the roof of the frat house, missing the pool, and hitting the concrete and reminding students that when they were responsible for the pool at the Sigma Nu house as Pool Commanders, it sparkled.

Despite the band songs and lack of current students attending the game, Georgia Tech's an outstanding school and we would be thrilled if any of our kids were accepted. Unfortunately, they won't be accepted because the AVERAGE ACT score is a 31.

DOCTORS AREN'T FUNNY

Peter works in the health field as a consultant to physician practices and hospital systems. Blah, blah, blah. He does acquisitions and improves efficiencies and the like. Peter's clients invite him to many social events that include spouses, and he declines 99 percent of them. He says, and I would agree, that sometimes I am an embarrassment.

During intermission at the ballet, we were buying a cocktail when a client of Peter's approached us, an internist that happened to look like a child molester.[59] He greeted Peter and then launched into an inquiry about laboratory equipment and fair market valuations and was still talking when the lights flickered, signaling that intermission was over.

The internist said to me, "I am so sorry for taking up the whole intermission with your husband when you two are on a date."

Believing my response was witty, I replied, "That's okay. We'll bill you." The physician gasped and stomped off.

The doctor will not return Peter's calls.

"You are welcome," I told Peter. Who would want a client that looks like a child molester AND is a such a stick in the mud?

---

[59] To my knowledge, the physician isn't an actual child molester.

AT LEAST I KEEP MY PANTIES ON

Peter, who hates to travel for business, accepted a travel speaking engagement to California, because it included two airline tickets and a weekend at the Four Seasons in Newport Beach. It was a lovely event, kicking off some sort of restructuring for a group of anesthesiologists. I enjoyed a massage at the spa and the drinks delivered to my chair on the beach while Peter attended meetings all day.

During dinner, they had a little rah-rah about accomplishments and goals and then everybody got to enjoy a nice meal of lobsters and pricey wine. For close to an hour, the five physicians at our table talked about regulatory change impacts and how Sugammadex is better for the reversal of neuromuscular blockade and how neostigmine is still more cost-effective when I turned to the doctor's wife beside me and said, "They really do make people sleepy." Peter, nor the physicians appreciated my anesthesiology humor.

Luckily, later in the night, my sleepy comment was all but forgotten due to the antics of "Naughty Nurse," Trashy,[60] the girlfriend of one of the physicians who worked as a nurse in the delivery room.

At first, she was being very flirty and playful because she knew most of the doctors from the hospital, but once the doctors'

---

[60] Not her real name.

wives were around, the physicians were not in the mood to reciprocate the racy banter of a bleached blond, double-D nurse wearing a skintight dress. Go figure.

Unfortunately, ignoring a naughty nurse is the absolute worst thing you can do to her. Trashy pouted and started downing the $100 bottles of Henri Puligny Montrachet Clos de la Mouchère[61] while snapping at the waitstaff to remove her "ugly white vegetables" (white asparagus).

Several Henri Puligny Montrachet Clos de la Mouchère bottles later, the group gathered in the hotel bar. A few of the physicians were calling it a night when Trashy tried to entice them to stay. At first, she tried to pour them another round, but when that did not work, she decided to shimmy out of her thong underwear and throw them around the group.

This was met with shock (women) and awe (men)—to her delight—so she took it up a notch. To her left was her boyfriend; to her right was a shy Columbian doctor. Trashy stood up and shimmered out of her thong panties and then wrapped them around the Columbian doctor's head and held them, with the triangle crotch portion over one of his eyes.

Trashy: You're a pirate!

Shy doctor: I am not a pirate. I am a physician.

Trashy: Noooooo, you're a pirate! He's a pirate, he's a pirate!

Shy doctor: I am not.

After a few rounds of "I'm not a pirate," the shy doctor, as well as all the guests except Trashy and her boyfriend, retired for the evening.

---

[61] Swanky white wine.

In the morning, the CEO, a lovely gentleman, stopped my husband and me in the hallway to address Trashy's antics. "I'm so embarrassed you had to see that last night. In the south, we call that white trash."

"That's what we call it in the north too," I informed him.

Trashy and the physician recently got married. They will have such a lovely story for their children.

A WEEKEND IN KIAWAH

Shortly after Peter and I were first married, we were invited to Kiawah Island to spend the weekend with Todd, one of his fraternity brothers, and his wife, Jennifer. [62] The Island is peppered with multimillion-dollar properties and a Hamptons-style clubhouse.

Two other couples were staying for the weekend and a few of their neighbors were planning to join us for a dinner party Todd and Jennifer were hosting Saturday night.

The morning of the party, Peter and the other guests went fishing. Jennifer and I wanted to lie out by their pool, listen to 1980s music and sip mojitos. We persuaded Todd to stay with us. After several hours of hanging by the pool and drinking mojitos, the theme song from *Dirty Dancing*, "(I've Had) The Time of My Life" came on the radio and Jennifer said, "Get in the pool, Todd, and catch Amy and I like Patrick Swayze did with Jennifer Grey."

Some men may have declined such a request but Jennifer is very sexy and assertive. Just a few hours earlier she was telling me about how a man in her neighborhood had been caught sleeping with his coworker and she yelled at Todd, "Try that, Todd, and I will cut your balls clean off," in her adorable, yet scary-at-the-time southern accent. So, Todd jumped in the pool

---

[62] Names changed.

and extended his arms. For about twenty minutes we took turns running and jumping and Todd would catch us while listing to the *Dirty Dancing* soundtrack.

Later, after we had cleaned up and had a fantastic dinner, everyone was drinking and having a great time when Cyndi Lauper's "Girls Just Want to Have Fun" came on. Jennifer encouraged all the ladies to come dance in the living room. After "Girls Just Want to Have Fun" was over, Prince's "When Doves Cry" blared and Jennifer performed a solo dance.

So, when Madonna's "Lucky Star" came on, the combination of the sun, the earlier Jennifer Grey moves and ten hours of mojitos gave me the confidence to do my own solo routine. I'm not a great dancer and I'm a terrible singer but I knew all the words and dance routines from Madonna's 1983 album *Madonna.* If you are over forty, you probably remember her routine—white studio, black plastic sunglasses, rolling around on the ground for over four minutes.

I grabbed a pair of sunglasses from the counter and started jumping around. In the middle of the song and a leg kick, I said, "Wow, this song is really long." Regardless, I was determined to finish. I started crawling on the ground and then rolling over, attempting Madonna's back-bend move. I finished by doing a split (not included in Madonna's video).

The crowd had mixed reviews- from confusion to pity. I was wearing white capri pants and had carpet burns so badly from crawling around that my knees bled through my jeans and onto their white carpet. I also pulled something in my back, but didn't feel it until the morning.

Sweet Jennifer and Todd still invite us to Kiawah. I'm not sure why, but Peter always says we have plans.

WELCOME TO HOLLYWOOD

A few months ago, I attended the American Film Market in Santa Monica. I had finished a screenplay, *#fakemom* (coming to a theater near you as soon as I sell it, and a studio agrees to make it). The AFM takes over Santa Monica, and every hotel and restaurant posts "Welcome AFM Attendees!" then jacks up their prices 50 percent for the week. Traci, my neighbor, grew up in LA and agreed to chauffer me around to all the activities.

The goal of the film market is to sell your film. The market is made up of independent filmmakers and my film is a mainstream comedy, so I was instructed to "just practice your pitch." (A pitch is a ten-second version of your film. For example, this is my film pitch: "It's a *Bridesmaids*-meets-*Bad Moms* female-centric comedy with a little romance and a lot of feel-good moments."

Traci and I picked up our $475-per-day[63] badges and proceeded to meet and mingle. We sat through parts of twenty films, SEVEN of which were foreign—Italian, Spanish, Polish, German, plus three Chinese films—hoping to spot my dream directors.[64] Often we were the only people in the theatre. At the end of our almost thousand-dollar day, the only people we had met were

---

[63] I work for a non-profit so $475.00 is a lot of money, to me.
[64] Elizabeth Banks, Reese Witherspoon, Ben Falcone, Judd Apatow and Paul Rudd.

the ticket takers and even they were not that excited to follow me on Twitter (@amylyle).

We weren't even trying to sell the film, just get the opportunity to pitch it, but everyone was super unapproachable,[65] heads down, on their phones or barking orders in Chinese. Apparently, China's richest man, Wang Jianlin, has been on a buying spree in Hollywood.

Traci and I had paid for industry passes, which entitled us to one cocktail party on the Santa Monica pier, so we slapped on some lipstick and headed in that direction. On the way, a gentleman, seeing our large AFM lanyards, stopped us and told us he "worked for Warner Brothers," and asked what films had we seen so far.

I heard "Warner Brothers" and belted out, "Let me buy you a beer!"

Traci and I sat at an outdoor bar and listened to Donald tell great movie stories. After about fifteen minutes he asked what we were doing at the market. I launched into an enthusiastic pitch of my movie, "It's like *Bridesmaids* meets *Bad Moms* ..."

He said he had not seen either of those films, but "it sounded great."

I asked him point-blank, "Who do you know at Warner Brothers and may I use your name?"

He paused, rubbed his chin and said, "Let me see, I knew Bernie and Walter. I worked in the accounting department from '56 to '63."

---

[65] Later, I found out I was on the wrong floor.

Traci yelled, "Check!" We shook hands with Accounting Don and moved on. "You have a real nose for people of influence," Traci threw out, correctly, as we headed for the pier.

The night before, at the beautiful Marina del Rey hotel, Traci and I were drinking our "free" cocktails (the rooms were $800) while film people swarmed around. You could distinguish the writers, wearing cute dresses and/or jeans, from the producers, sporting suits and ties. Traci encouraged me to mingle with the crowd when (1) my cocktail kicked in, and (2) two gentleman in suits approached us and asked, "How'd you do today?"

I stuck out my hand, said, "Great!" and launched into my pitch: "Imagine *Bridesmaids* meets *Bad Moms* … a female-centric comedy…" The guys in the suits said that the film sounded fantastic. I was so excited to finally get to pitch to real producers so I bravely asked, "Want to join us?"

The two suits sat down. I launched into a five-minute synopsis of the film, who I wanted to produce it, and my dream cast. They kept saying, "That sounds so incredible."

I thanked them and asked, "Are you guys having any luck at the film market?"

They looked at each other and said in unison, "We sell lamps," and handed us their business cards. They were from Idaho visiting LA to attend an architectural convention to pitch their very expensive lamps. Traci laughed until she cried.

I spent about $3000 for the weekend and my only real pitch was to lamp salesmen.

NOT THAT THERE IS ANYTHING WRONG WITH THAT

During the film festival weekend, I met Traci's family and got a personal tour of LA. Traci drove me down the street of my favorite movie of all times, *Bridesmaids*. It's the scene where Kristen Wiig finally realizes that she's worth more than a one night stand with the super-hot but sleazy Ted, played by Jon Hamm. Traci obliged me when I wanted to see the famous Dolby Theatre (where the Academy Awards have been hosted for the past forty years) and she drove me by the famous "Hollywood" sign on the hill. She even slowed to a crawl so I could jump out of the car and take a picture with the sidewalk stars on Sunset Strip.

The closest I've made it any Hollywood stars.

Downtown Hollywood is super-congested with traffic so it takes about an hour to travel a block. By the time our sightseeing was ending, it was after six and we were starving. We parked and went to Enclave, a nice indoor/outdoor cafe in West Hollywood.

We struck up a conversation with two nice ladies sitting next to us and found out they were native LA and shared a mutual friend with Traci. We told them we were at the American Film Market and they asked about the film.

I started my "female-driven comedy" spiel when they exclaimed, "Female comedy? That's so great! We're lesbians!"

I was thrown off and blurted, "It's not a lesbian comedy. It just has women in it. I guess they could be lesbians but I hadn't thought about it." Traci kicked me under the table and shut me up.

Traci, always calm and appropriate, talked about her sister who had recently lost her (same-sex) partner. They nodded in understanding and sympathy and then looked to me. I personally don't know any lesbians, but I am a real girl's girl and if I ever moved out of the suburbs, I'm quite sure I would hang out with plenty of lesbians.

Anywho, they keep looking at me as if to ask, "What do you, girl from small-town Ohio, think about lesbians?" Although I suffer from misophonia and was annoyed by plenty of noises, I also suffer from sedatephobia,[66] which means the worst sound of all ... silence. I'm sure it was only a few seconds, but it felt like ten minutes, with everyone staring at me.

---

[66] All my conditions are self-diagnosed from WebMD and television commercials.

I panicked and started naming every lesbian I could think of. "I love Ellen DeGeneres, Paula Poundstone, Wanda Sykes, Rosie O'Donnell, Jodie Foster and two of my favorite writers are lesbians, Virginia Woolf AND Carson McCullers. Carson wrote that book about the deaf mute.[67] I'm considering getting a Subaru because they are super dependable." Our two new friends and Traci continued to stare at me so I continued, "I would totally be a lesbian. I love women and tidiness, plus we could share clothes but I can't because the thought of going down on lady-parts really gets my gagger."

After a long pause, Traci and the two ladies burst out laughing. We shared our desserts over an in-depth debate over trickle-down versus trickle-up economics (we were weeks away from the Clinton/Trump election). And then, before we left, they threw out, "We should give Amy our friend Dee's contact information." When I asked who Dee was, they answered, "A content director of Amazon."

I love people that give you a second chance and judge you on your heart and intentions.

---

[67] *The Heart is a Lonely Hunter*

NOT TONIGHT, HONEY

My husband and I have been arguing about sex since we got married. He says, "Women want sex just as much as men." His logic is that 50 percent of married men cheat and they are cheating with women, so it must be equal.

A few married women do go through a super-slutty period when they are in a crisis. Normally, they're on the brink of a nasty divorce and lash out by sleeping with the low hanging fruit husbands in their own neighborhoods or offices. These husbands are the ones that have been prowling around, cheating on their wives for their entire marriages. I've witnessed this behavior in my old neighborhood and an entire cul-de-sac ended up getting divorced.

How many times have you heard a man say, "My wife is an animal—she wants it all the time?" Never, that's how often. (If you are a woman reading this and thinking, *I can't get enough sex from my husband,* and you're not a newlywed, good for you. You have some sort of extra hormones that most of us lack.)

My girlfriends and I talk about sex frequently and it seems that most women *want to want to* have sex but after taking care of the kids and/or working all day, have no mojo. If we try to be generous and agree to sex, the hubbies still complain, "You're acting like you're not that into it." Gentleman, that's not acting. If we don't even get credit for having sex without being acrobats, that makes us even less likely to comply. It becomes a vicious no hanky panky cycle.

My sex excuse list:

Ate too much	It's still daylight
Haven't brushed my teeth	You were mean to me earlier
It's Monday for God's sake	I was asleep!
Didn't sleep well	I just changed the sheets
Just not feeling it	The kids are still awake
My legs aren't shaved	I ate dairy
My nails are still wet	I must finish this chapter
It's Sunday!	You need to manscape
I just ate garlic	Did you eat curry for lunch?
Backache	I have to finish a work project
Stomachache	I think the dog wants out
Headache	I think the dog wants in
You drank too much	Is someone at the door?
I haven't drunk enough	I have to get up early
Let me watch the rest of this show	Didn't we just do it?
Not in the mood	I'm so tired
I have a charley horse in my leg	I need to change the laundry
I haven't showered	I think I'm pre-menopausal

Men seem to be more visually stimulated than women. If women are in an elevator and an attractive man steps in, they're probably thinking, *I bet that suit is a Stanley Korshak—it looks expensive.* They're not wondering about the gentleman's penis size or visualizing copulation.

My final piece of evidence about men and women not wanting sex equally is this: ask 100 women how much they spent on the four billion dollars' worth of pornography sold last year in the US. Ninety-nine percent would say "Zero." [68]

---

[68] Please send me your sex excuses, they may make the sequel. www.amylyle.me

AND IT'S NOT EVEN EIGHT AM

I walked past Peter shaving, in the shower.

Peter: Ouch! This razor is so dull. Have you been using it again on your legs?

Me: No. I used it on my lady parts.

Peter: I asked you not to use my razor. It dulls it and then rips my face off.

Me: Did you know that you have a slight lisp?

Peter: What?

Me: Yes. You said, "dullths" and "ripths." That's a lisp. Did you go to speech therapy as a child, because you should have.

Peter: Why is it when I catch you doing something that I asked you not to do, you launch a personal attack?

Me: Do you hear yourself? You said, "perthonal." You should get that checked out. Is your tongue swollen?

Peter: Oh my God, you are so weird.

THEY GET INTO ALL THE CREVICES

To celebrate my friend Amanda's birthday, we went to Jeju Sauna Korean Spa. In Atlanta, we have pockets that are predominantly Korean with restaurants serving bibimbap and shabu-shabu, several Korean karaoke bars and warehouse sized spas.

Plan to stay at a Korean spa for the day as there're countless treatments and activities to do. After checking in, you're issued blue scrubs, not unlike what your dental hygienist would wear, and a towel. A tour guide of sorts walks you through the facility. In the open area, they have a variety of spas that resemble igloos.

Spas available:

Wood Sauna: Traditional warm sauna that reduces tension and opens pores

Baked Clay: Dilates peripheral blood vessels and helps eliminate waste products

Jade: Infused with herbs, increases metabolism and relieves arthritis

Gold and Silver: Helps with nerve stability and neurosis

Jewels: Lined with semiprecious stones, offers calming powers and "mind-glowing powers"

Rock Ice: Lowers your body temperature and contracts the pores

Charcoal: Toxin absorbing and stimulates sweat glands

Each spa could hold ten to twenty people, but many were unoccupied and very peaceful. Amanda and I did encounter one gentleman reading Dante in the jade igloo and another in a headstand yoga pose in the baked-clay igloo. The floor is heated throughout the spa, making it very comfortable to wander around in bare feet.

Entering the locker room to change, you'll catch sight of hundreds of naked women speaking different languages, from Spanish to Swahili. You wear your scrubs if you choose to travel to the mix-sexed areas; otherwise, you remain au naturel.

As we were leaving the locker room for our treatment, we passed a small room with a glass door where we could see a few women sitting on low stools wrapped in long black capes. Attendants were putting what looked like spaghetti pots of hot water under their stools. Our guide explained that the ladies were getting chai-yok—their vaginas steamed. It's an ancient treatment that reduces stress, fights infections, regulates menstrual cycles, balances female hormone levels, aids in infertility and clears hemorrhoids. Additives like wormwood, lemon or lavender can be added to the V-steam if you would like your vajayjay to be scented as such.

Amanda and I thought about doing the Chai-yok treatment but the ladies sitting on the crotch pots looked ashamed. Perhaps they had a Groupon and misunderstood chai-yok to be an exotic yoga class. We moved on to our treatments.

The first phase required us to alternate soaking in hot tubs and cold tubs for several minutes each. Then it was time for ... THE SCRUB.

Lined up in military fashion were ten to fifteen stainless-steel cadaver-style tables. Completely naked, you lie on the table while an older Korean woman wearing military-issue-looking underpants-and-bra set starts dumping buckets of water on your body. Amanda described it as "waterboarding."

Scrubbing table

Next, the women put on scrubby mitts and scoured us like we were dirty potatoes. As sheets of dead skin fell from the mitts, we were slipping and sliding on the tables. Just when I thought I could not take one more second of the Brillo-pad treatment, the buckets of water started again. I had my eyes closed but could hear other women spit and spatter as they tried to catch their breath. Then ... silence and the smell of deliciously fresh cucumbers that the attendants had grated by hand. They placed the fresh cucumber gently on our faces. Last, they massaged our scalps for twenty minutes and washed our hair.

Remaining naked, we shuffled into the shower to rinse off. We were exhausted and needed food. The Jeju offers an authentic Korean restaurant, so we enjoyed fresh fish and noodles while sitting on floor cushions at the low platforms and watching other people explore the healing igloos.

We would have loved to have rested in their nap room, gotten a Ji-ap reflexology massage and taken a dip in their mineral pool, but we had to head home to get our kids off the bus.

The amazing, all-day adventure at Jeju Spa is around $50.

IT'S MY FACE

My mother (and Oscar Wilde) said, "Youth is wasted on the young." I knew not to do all the things that would age me, such as baking in the sun, not getting enough sleep and drinking alcohol, but I didn't listen. Hence, I'm looking more and more like an old lady.

Some of it is genetics (this orange-peel-like texture running down the sides of my legs must have come from my grandmother). Certainly, gravity plays a role—how else could you explain butt cheeks changing from the shape of coconuts to something tubular? You've seen it at the beach: the eighty-year-old guy in a Speedo, holding a metal detector, with *Florida-old-man cheeks*. We are all are destined for this if we don't start doing excruciatingly painful lunges and the exercise Satan himself invented—squats. I don't do either and now shorts are a thing of the past.

At forty-five, I'm not going to look any better. Therefore, I started buying shimmery/sparkly clothing—to distract people from my face.

Other atrocities I'm experiencing:

- My hair has turned into wire, resembling a combination of Animal, the crazy drummer from The Muppets, and the 1970s *SNL* character Roseanne Roseannadanna.
- Back/knee/neck pains that used to go away with one glass of wine or a Tylenol are not going away.
- Extra pounds will not come off.

- No energy.
- Random black, coarse hairs—mostly above my lip but sometimes I find them on my chin or on one of my nipples.
- Extreme paleness of skin.
- Brown spots are appearing all over my body.
- Even darker circles under my eyes.
- Blindness. The other day I ate what I thought was a Reese Pieces at the bottom of my purse but it was an Advil tablet.
- My eyeballs are changing shape, getting narrower and smaller. This is really bad news as I have somewhat beady eyeballs already.
- Giant pores—magnification mirrors are no friend to me.

My mornings start with fifteen minutes of vitamin and supplement swallowing.

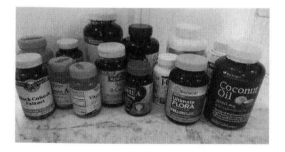

- Fish Oil – Healthy heart
- Ultimate Flora – Healthy bacteria, promotes good digestive health (a miracle supplement if you can't poop or poop too much)
- Black Cohosh Extract – Menopause support
- Vitamin D – Immune health
- Vitamin A – Essential for healthy skin

- DHEA – Promotes a balanced hormone level (anti-bitch pills)
- Super B Complex – Cellular energy and antioxidant support
- Vitamin C – Supports immune function
- Turmeric Curcumin – Fights and potentially reverses diseases
- Osteo Bi- Flex – Strengthens your joints, reduces joint pain
- Lutein and Zeaxanthin – Eye health
- Strontium – Improves bone density
- Ribose – For energy and mental clarity
- Hydrochloric Acid – Reduces bloating
- Green tea – Improves brain function; encourages fat loss; lowers risk of cancer, Alzheimer's, Parkinson's, and cardiovascular disease; decreases your risk of dying and improves dental health

Getting old is expensive.

I MAY NOT BE ABLE TO HELP YOU

I moved to the south after I graduated from college and found work as an administrator (glamorous for receptionist) during the week and worked at Rich's Department store evenings and weekends. Rich's had a long history with Atlanta, as it had opened in 1867 and for over a century had been "The" place to shop. When Martin Luther King Jr. received the Nobel Peace Prize in Oslo, Norway, in 1964, he was wearing a coat that his wife, Coretta Scott King, had bought for him from the downtown Atlanta Rich's Department Store.

Famous for their personal-shopper services and generous return policies (they allowed people to return anything, even if it the item had not been bought in their stores, for cash), and although they were founded by Jewish immigrants, they were most famous for their Christmas festivities. The lighting of the "Great Tree," a massive pine displayed on the store's rooftop, was a huge Atlanta attraction. Another Rich's seasonal favorite was The Pink Pig train that looped around The Great Tree.

In preparation for the tree lighting, the well-heeled women of Atlanta would need to retrieve their fur coats from Rich's fur vault. It's only cold in Atlanta about ninety days of the year, but by God, if people in Chicago and Manhattan were draped in fur, the fine ladies of Atlanta would be too. I was fascinated by our customers strolling around the store in their $10,000 chinchilla stoles and minks trimmed with fox furs.

The busiest "fur rush" at Rich's was after church on Sundays. I grew up in Ohio, where going to church (or whatever religion you were) was a private matter—not the case in Atlanta. Every Sunday the fur-clad ladies would ask me, "Honey did you attend service this morning?" I would reply that no, I had to work on the weekends. Southern ladies are sweet as sugar but ruthless in uncovering your standing with the Lord. "When you are not working, where does your family attend church?" Or they would boldly ask me, "Where are you on your walk with Jesus?" They would be very offended when I told them I wasn't attending, but they would offer, "I will be praying for your soul." I said to a coworker that I would be praying for the souls of the 150 chinchillas that were murdered for their full-length pelts.

I was fired from Rich's—not because of my walk with the Lord or my mockery of the PETA offenders, but for a "returns violation." I showed up for my shift to work in accessories that day, and they redirected me to the lingerie department because a few people had called out sick.

A woman approached the lingerie counter and asked about our return policy. As I mentioned, Rich's had a super-liberal return policy and the only restriction I can remember was that you could not return bathing suits or lingerie if the item had been worn. (Rich's put restrictions on those returns only because it

192

was a state law.) I showed the lady the posted sign and said, "We can accept any returns except on lingerie or bathing suits if the tags have been removed or if the item has been worn."

The woman told me the item had not been worn, pulled a hot-pink silky tank top and matching shorts that smelled like cigarettes, cheap perfume and sweat from her purse, and set them on the counter.

I said, "Ma'am (in the south you say *ma'am*), there are no tags on this item." The customer dug around in her purse and slapped the tags on the counter. A line had started to form behind me, as this was Sunday and the fur ladies were either buying, retrieving or showing off their furs while they Christmas shopped. I said, "I am so sorry but we cannot accept lingerie that has been worn."

The customer went nuts, screaming and cursing that she had been a customer of Rich's for over twenty years and she had never been treated so poorly. She demanded to see the manager. When my manager arrived and asked what the issue was, the customer said, "Your salesgirl said I can't return this item because it's been worn. I bought this item and I know for a fact it hasn't been worn."

My manager gave me a "And your reply?" look, so I took a pen and delicately lifted the pink silky shorts. It felt like the entire store had stopped to watch as a pair of black lacy panties dropped to the counter.

"These have been worn," I said.

Later in the office, my sweet manager said, "You embarrassed a loyal Rich's customer."

The words that I needed to say ("I'm so sorry") refused to materialize. I said, "I think she embarrassed herself," and clocked out.

TRYING TO GIVE BACK

I wanted the kids to be involved in a philanthropic activity on a monthly basis. Anna wanted to help the people in Africa, PJ's in Boy Scouts and suggested clothing drives, Savannah's passion was to help the elderly in our community and Maddy was most interested in serving the homeless. As per the norm in my household, a heated battle erupted over who to help. I suggested we help animals. Remarkably, everyone agreed.

The Forsyth County Animal Shelter is only a few miles from our house and allows children to assist with cleaning cat cages and walking the dogs. We arrived at the shelter and told them we were there to help with the dogs. The employee immediately assumed we were there to adopt a dog, which got the kids all excited and then crushed when I reminded them that we were only WALKING the dogs.

Each of the four kids picked out an animal. Anna, only five or six at the time, picked out a large husky, Savannah selected a Lab, Maddy picked a small terrier/beagle mix and PJ picked what the lady said was a "chiweenie." The lady put looped leashes around each of the dogs and told us where the "walk zones" were behind the building. Less than one minute after getting the kids outside, they wanted me to take a picture.

Savannah's Labrador didn't want to be in the group picture I was taking. While trying to lift him, he wiggled free and ran away. All the kids started crying, and the dog was nowhere in sight. I took the sobbing kids back into the shelter and explained the situation.

The shelter employee said to her coworker, "They lost one of our f****** dogs." I apologized profusely and scooted the children out of the shelter and into the car.

Less than a mile up the road, we saw the escaped Labrador. Savannah opened the door and whistled; it ran as fast as it could and jumped into the car. I drove back to the shelter, returned the dog, and asked if we could come back next month to walk the dogs. The shelter employee said that we were no longer allowed to walk the dogs but we could return if we wanted to clean cat cages. No good deed goes unpunished.[69]

---

[69] Oscar Wilde

If your spouse asks you, "Why do you love me" and you reply, "You have a fairly good driving record and white teeth." Please know, that is not what they are looking for.

WOMEN'S RIGHTS

The elementary school does a great job of bringing history alive every year with the "Wax Museum" exhibit. Kids research historically significant people, select a favorite, and then dress up and memorize a one- to two-minute speech. When the parents show up for the exhibit, hundreds of students are "frozen," representing everyone from Harriet Tubman to Neil Armstrong. Each student has a homemade "button" next to them that the parents push to make the wax figure come to life.

It was impressive to go down each row and listen to the speeches of the Founding Fathers, past presidents, and inventors of the United States.

I explored the "Important Women in History" section first and pushed the button of a little girl sporting a black wig with a severe part. She started her speech: "I wrote many short stories under the pen name A. M. Barnard, but I'm most famous for writing the novel *Little Women*. I'm Louisa May Alcott. I'm unique because I was born in 1832 but was the breadwinner, which means I supported my whole family, and I NEVER GOT MARRIED, EVER."

Wax museum Rosa Parks sat for her presentation as a symbol of her 1965 refusal to give up her bus seat for a white man. She beautifully explained "I had been denied the right to education and how she was not in a struggle of black versus white but a struggle of right versus wrong."[70]

I heard several young ladies quoting Elizabeth Cady Stanton and Susan B. Anthony regarding the importance of women's suffrage. My favorite by far was the passionate rendition of Abigail Adams. "Remember the ladies," a colonial-dressed little girl scolded, "and be more generous and favorable to them than your ancestors. Do not put such unlimited power into the hands of the husbands." She was rewarded with applause by many parents.

I then headed to the "Important Men in History" section, which featured many as George Washington, Benjamin Franklin and Paul Revere. As I listened to the fourth and fifth graders recite what they viewed as the most important aspects of our country's great men, I noticed a theme. It went something like this ...

"I'm a Founding Father of the United States, commander in chief, the republic's first president. I am George Washington. My father was a tobacco farmer but my mother had no occupation. I had six siblings."

Or ...

"I, Benjamin Franklin, was a Founding Father of the United States, a printer, and the inventor of bifocals, the lightning rod, and carriage odometer. My mother did not work. I was one of eight children. My father was a soap maker."

And ...

---

[70] Taken from the 1965 Montgomery, Alabama, speech

"I, Paul Revere, was famous for alerting the colonial militia that THE BRITISH ARE COMING! I was a patriot and industrialist. My father was a blacksmith. My mother had twelve children, but she did not have a job."

Ninety percent of the kids probably just cut and pasted from Wikipedia and that is how the site describes women but the comments about women surprised everyone.

The parents and the teachers started asking the boys, "Twelve children and you said she didn't work, really?" and "The woman was on a farm and had eight kids. Tell me how that is not work. Do you understand how difficult that would be? They didn't even have washing machines. She may have had to kill her own chicken for dinner. How dare you ... do you think I don't work? Who made your lunch? Who takes you to ball practice? Who?"

I suppose in textbook language this would be labeled as *Progressing the Perception of Women*. It takes a village.

I WOULD JUST DIE

When Savannah started middle school, she was pretty confident until the fourth day. Running late from the locker room to get to gym class, she turned and slammed the corner of her shirt into her locker. As she headed to the gym, she snapped back like a rubber band, crashing herself into her locker. She flopped to the floor. After several minutes of yelling for help, another student came to her rescue, opening the combination lock to free her.

I asked Savannah, "Why didn't you just slide out of your shirt and undo your locker yourself?"

Her eyes lit up in horror. "Mom! That would be too embarrassing."

WE NEED PROFESSIONAL HELP

When Peter and I got married, we had no idea how difficult it would be to blend families. Although we bought several "how to blend'" books, we didn't believe that WE would have any of the issues the books listed:

- Sibling rivalry
- Scheduling issues
- Ex-spouse issues or
- Being able to tolerate each other's children

Peter and I returned from our honeymoon and within two weeks we were having issues with:

- Sibling rivalry
- Scheduling issues
- Ex-spouse issues and
- Being able to tolerate each other's children

We went to counseling. Counselor number one would bat her eyelashes fifteen times and then close her eyes while she listened. When Peter and I finished talking, her eyes remained closed for so long; we never knew if she was in deep contemplation or asleep. Unfortunately, regardless what our issues were regarding the children, her response was always the same: "Why is that important to you?" It didn't matter if we were talking about the kids' grades, making curfew, or being responsible for doing chores. She would take a huge breath, close her eyes and say, "Why is that important to you?"

I respect the field of psychology, and "Why is that important to you?" might have been a legitimate question if we were having issues with someone over spending or drinking too much, but having kids make their beds? It's important to us because we want the kids to learn responsibility and respect. I wanted to say "It's important that the kids do a few chores now, so they won't be complete a**holes as adults. Finally, I told Peter that we were not paying someone $150 an hour to question "why" we want what we want. I need more advice on "how" to get what we want.

Peter and I selected our own counselors for the second round. Peter went to someone he used to know and I went to a female therapist that a friend had recommended. Counselor number two did provide me with some invaluable advice: "You cannot control other people; you can only control yourself." This is very true but hard to remember when you are running a household with so many people.

I stopped going to counselor number two because she kept projecting NEW and WORSE issues onto me and the kids.

Session One

Counselor: Tell me about your father.

Me: I'm here to talk about my new marriage and blended family.

Counselor: What was your father's personality like?

Me: Um ... he was controlling but we have a good relationship now.

Counselor: Are you depressed?

Me: No.

Counselor: Depression isn't sadness- do you lack energy or the will to do things? getting out of bed or spending time with other people?

Me: No, I'm not depressed.

Counselor: Would you be ashamed to admit you were depressed? I have issues with depression and it was very hard for me to admit it.

Me: Ten years ago, when I got divorced, I was very depressed. I'm not ashamed of it. I'm not here because I'm depressed and would like to spend our time talking about the new marriage and the ...

Counselor: Many people tell themselves that they're not depressed, because they think it is a weakness.

Me: I don't think having depression is a weakness. I have a lot of issues, depression is just not one of them. My issue, right now, is how I can better deal with a blended family.

Counselor: Hmm.

Session five

Me: I would like to improve communication with the children.

Counselor: They children are disobedient?

Me: Yes, they are normal kids, but we are having some issues with the kids being disobedient and not being respectful. We'd like to improve our relationship with them.

Counselor: Are the children depressed?

Me: What?

Counselor: The children, do they avoid social interaction, have low energy or say they have violent thoughts?

Me: No.

Counselor: How do you know?

Me: They are very social and have never said anything about being depressed.

Counselor: Maybe they are scared to tell you. I felt depressed and was scared to tell anyone until my 20's.

Me: I know, you shared that with me a couple of times now, and I'm so sorry that you struggle with that. Did you want to talk more about your depression?

> Counselor talks about various medications and which ones worked for her.

Me: I'm glad that helped.

Counselor: Do you think medication would help you or your kids?

Me: I'm not sure about that, I think we just need to work on understanding one another.

Counselor: Do you want me to evaluate them for depression?

Me: Exhales loudly.

The counselor scribbles into her notebook.

Millions of people benefit from counseling and I'm sure I would benefit from counseling if I could find the right counselor.[71]

Until then, I'll just keep writing these weird stories.

---

[71] Clinical depression is a major depressive disorder and should be treated by a medical professional.

CRUSHING YOUR PARENTS

When my sister and I were taking swimming lessons at the YMCA, we caught the eye of swim coach Bill Bauer. My parents liked the idea of us exerting our energy in the pool, instead of at each other. Swimming instills discipline, confidence, and as my father said, "it will substantially reduce your chances of drowning." We were enrolled to join the Marietta Marlins.

Swim meets are long affairs that drag on from eight in the morning until oftentimes late into the evening, for entire weekends. There's a lot of waiting around at swim meets as there may be an hour between events.

I quit swimming altogether at the most inopportune time, when I was a senior in high school and the swim coaches were introducing me to college coaches.

An average daily swim workout is over two thousand yards.

2,000 yards five days a week = 10,000 yards every week = 480,000 yards annually x 12 years =

FIVE MILLION, SEVEN HUNDRED SIXTY THOUSAND YARDS

Five million yards was enough swimming. My parents handled it well considering that they had also put in twelve years. "You are wasting your talent," was my father's only comment.

SQUIRREL SLAYER

My friend Katie,[72] an art director and magazine columnist, ranks in the top five of my favorite friends. When you think of Katie, you think "lovely." She has an amazing eye for design, is funny and looks like a supermodel. With all of this in mind, I was surprised to learn that Kathleen had shot a caged squirrel in her attic.

Katie and her husband had been trying to evict the squirrels for months, cutting down branches close to the house, using scent repellents and installing the Ultrasonic Rodent Repeller that gives off a high-frequency sound squirrels detest. The squirrels would not relocate. They were making nests, eating the wood and shorting out electrical wires.

The night Katie's husband left for a work trip, she was awakened by a horrific racket. When she pulled down the attic stairs and climbed high enough to grab the single light bulb string that was dangling from the ceiling, she spotted a squirrel, hurling itself against a metal trap, yipping and snarling.

Over lunch we discussed the assassination:

Me: I thought you said it was a catch-and-release cage. Why didn't you put it outside?

---

[72] Name changed.

Katie: It was growling and throwing itself against the cage. I'm pretty sure it was rabid.

Me: At what moment did you decide to execute it?

Katie: The second I saw its beady eyeballs.

Me: You shot him?

Katie: Yes. You know how much I need my f****** sleep.

Me: With a shotgun?

Katie: That would go through our house, Amy. I shot him with my son's Daisy Red Ryder BB gun.

Me: From what range?

Katie: At least fifteen feet, I was trying to stay balanced on the attic ladder and fire at the same time.

Me: Are you a good shot?

Katie: No. It took about forty-five minutes. I had to take a break to reload to finish him off.

Me: Then you put the cage outside?

Katie: No, I went to bed. In morning, I called Varmint Guard and they removed the corpse and applied an antimicrobial treatment to the attic.

Me: Hmm. I find the whole series of events fascinating.

Katie: I hate f****** squirrels.

FREUDIAN SLIP

I signed up for a ten-week improv class. Seth, our hilariously gifted instructor, lectured the new improv troop (Team Monday!) that the goal of improv was to get to the "iceberg level." Seth explained Freud's theory of how our minds have three different levels:

> The conscious mind – the rational part of our brains; the top of the iceberg

> The preconscious mind – the part of our brain that holds our memories that we pull into consciousness when we need to; the part of the iceberg that you can still see, just below the water surface

> The unconscious mind – the part of the brain that is a reservoir of feelings, thoughts, urges, and memories outside our conscious awareness; the part of the iceberg that is hidden, deep below the surface

Every week we learned different strategies to hone our performances: accepting and advancing, mirror versus foil, raising the stakes, tagging out, etc. We applied these to a gamut of pretend situations, such as visiting the doctor, vacation-pictures slideshow, conducting circus/stripper/fast-food job interviews, getting arrested, a breakup, criminals on the run, waking up with amnesia, giving a eulogy at the wrong funeral, and strange-foods cooking show.

210

After ten weeks, I was still the worse improviser of our group. I would completely freeze in the moment. I knew my issues stemmed from trying to plan a funny scene—the kiss of death in improv. As Seth says, you must clear your mind and let your UNCONSCIOUS mind loose.

Only a few times did I ever get to the coveted "unconscious zone," and I never want to go back. I kept having a theme of the same thoughts, words and physical outbursts. Regardless of whether the scene was a pretend cooking show or two people on an airplane, I would start babbling about midgets, listing sexually transmitted diseases and pretending to punch my teammates in the throat.

What does that say about me as a person? Why would my mind go to such an awful place? It is a total coincidence that midgets, STDs and mock punching people in the throat worked fairly well in improv and was appreciated by the audience but I was mortified by exposing what I suppose is my dark side.

DO NOT MOVE MY CHEESE

An ironic result of being raised in a completely chaotic and unstable environment is that as an adult I have developed the need for complete control and stability. No evidence proves that parenting styles cause obsessive-compulsive disorder, but no studies prove they don't.

If you are wondering *Do I have OCD?* and keep wondering about it for over an hour, you have OCD. Welcome to the club! OCD impacts everybody differently. Like all my issues, I try to see the advantages of the condition and add a positive spin: *I'm thorough and tidy!*

I am overly concerned about the following:

- The symmetry of all things: bushes, lamps, Roman shades
- Routines: bedtime, working out, reading magazines back to front—there's a *process*.
- Appliance checks: Our poor neighbors get calls, *Will you make sure the dryer, straightening irons and oven are turned off?*
- Trash in the indoor trash cans: *Where should the trash be?* you may ask. It goes to the outside trash cans, frequently.
- The sink: Seeing dirty dishes in the sink makes my mind race. *Why are those in the sink? Why aren't they in the dishwasher? Wait a minute, I bet the*

dishwasher is full and the kids forgot to unload it. They are trying to drive me mad!

- Everything needs to be counted: nails in a deck, squares on the ceiling, the pores on my nose
- I'm not a good counter: If there is something of volume, I'll count it 10 times and still not be confident that I have the right number.
- Rug tassels: They need to be perfectly straight. I cut the tassels off our rugs because both my husband and I suffer from the twisted-tassel issue.
- Cleaning: *Overzealous* would be an understatement.
- Items need their own sections: Sports bras, pretty bras, strapless bras, ugly bras, racerback bras and sticky boobs are in separate drawers.

Dream closet

- Clutter: No. Never.
- Having OCD: *Do people think I'm crazy? Do they? Do they? Do they?*

If you suffer from a severe case, you have options: drugs and/or therapy. When my mind starts obsessing, I stop and try to recite (in my head) my Sunday actor gig scripts, which seems to get me back on track.

If you want to give a person with OCD joy, send them a photo from @OCDthings on Twitter. It offers thousands of photographs of impeccably arranged, ordered and stacked items, like this giant box of crayons where each crayon is facing the same direction in their own section, light to dark.

In this chaotic world ... it is perfect.

DOG DAYS

Cooper and I walk every day in our neighborhood. As we made our morning loop, we spotted our new neighbor's dog, Jimmy Chews. He's a labradoodle and was head to tail in mud playing by the lake. Jimmy Chews' muddy state panicked the family getting Christmas pictures taken (all dressed up) near the lake.

Trying to be helpful, I grabbed Jimmy Chews by the collar and dragged him toward his yard. Meanwhile, Cooper, who is not fixed because my husband declares he "would never be responsible for cutting the balls off another male," is shamelessly attempting to hump Jimmy Chews.

As I schlepped Jimmy Chews to his yard Cooper still vigorously gyrating, I heard "What the f*** are you doing? Let go of my dog!" I turned to see Jimmy Chews' owner, enraged by what looked to her to be the forced breeding of her animal.

"I was returning him to your yard," I explained.

She jerked Jimmy Chews' collar, releasing him from Cooper's sexual attack, and turned him loose. Jimmy Chews immediately jumped back into the lake and then to the fleeing Christmas-photo family to shake.

"We let him play in the pond," was all Jimmy Chews' mom said and went back inside.

Jimmy Chews and family have since moved and are thriving in the suburbs of Birmingham.

LAKE LIFE

When my hubby was a teenager, he helped build a cabin with his brothers on Lake Hartwell, which is positioned on the border of Georgia and South Carolina. Many lakes in Georgia suffer from zoning issues, the biggest issue being there is no zoning. At Hartwell, you can find a gated, million-dollar house next to a broken-down trailer that has *If you step foot on my property I will shoot you* spray-painted on the side of it.

After a two-year drought in Georgia, the water level, as well as lake-property prices, was at an all-time low. So of course, that's the time we put the property on the market.

Peter's dad was a hoarder[73] and the basement of the property was filled with junk. My husband is more of a delegator of work than the doer of work when it comes to cleaning out basements, so he stayed busy walking the property with a surveyor while the kids and I purged.

Several times he would come to the basement, waving *a treasure* he had found in the dumpster. "Why would you throw this away?" he would ask, regarding boxes of waterlogged tax records from the 1940s and a collection of broken Eastern Airline lowball glasses.

We booked ourselves for several weekends at the cabin to clean and to meet all the contractors coming to fix windows, re-grout showers and install new appliances. I was in the kitchen when

---

[73] Peter insists his father is a *collector*.

the refrigerator was being delivered from Home Depot. Trying to make small talk, I asked, "Besides Home Depot, where do people work around here?"

Refrigerator installer shared with me, "Some folks work at Gumlog Barbeque. It's owned by a man named Doodlebug. That's an alias, Doodlebug. Word is he's wanted by the law for running white lightning. We have the Swamp Guinea, a catfish place and there are a few chicken farms." He paused for a second as he wrestled the refrigerator into the cabinet. "Mostly there are methamphetamine labs and dog-fighting rings."

After several months, the cabin finally sold. The next day, it started to rain.

WHAT HAPPENS IN FLORIDA

Lil,[74] a friend of mine since high school who worked as a teacher and needed a break from her two small kids, invited me to go on a weekend spa vacation in St. Augustine. We got settled and enjoyed a nice day at the beach and then headed to a great stone-crab restaurant in town that a fellow guest had recommended.

We were sitting at the bar, sipping our cocktails, when a group of girls in their twenties entered the bar. They were tan and beautiful in their cutoff shorts, tank tops and long, blond hair. Lil and I looked at each other in our bright floral outfits and bob haircuts and felt very old.

Seated outside for dinner, we could see the group of girls being wild and having a great time. "We're so old—let's do something crazy," Lil suggested as she placed her shrimp tails neatly to one side of her plate. The craziest thing Lil and I had ever done was getting our ears double-pierced in seventh grade.

"Like what?" I asked, thinking for a second about how I did have a recurring dream of hog-tying a delivery guy and crashing the truck through the front window of a Louis Vuitton store so I could have all the clothes, handbags and sunglasses.

"Amy!" Lil snapped me out of my fantasy. "Look."

---

[74] Name changed.

An old Camaro had pulled into the parking lot with an ad for a tattoo parlor on the top, like a pizza delivery car. It was a sign.

You would think that two thirty-year-old ladies wearing Lily Pulitzer sundresses walking into a tattoo/piercing parlor would evoke looks of reproach, but the tattoo artists simply said cheerfully, "Pick your design," and handed us photo albums of tattoos.

I stood in front of a mirror and tried to envision something that I would want FOREVER on my body. Did I want a tiny turtle on my hip or maybe a significant word like *Grace* or *Hope* in a script style under my armpit? As an artist called Lil over and started preparing her with rubbing alcohol, I flipped through a Chinese dictionary and I selected the symbol for strength and confidence, two things I believe you need when getting a tattoo.

I told the artist I would like the dime-sized tattoo on the inside of my foot, by my ankle bone.

He said, "No one will be able to see it there."

I said, "I know."

With great trepidation, I eventually agreed to a tiny tattoo on the outside of my left foot. My mind was racing back and forth: *Will it show when I wear work shoes?* and although I was thirty, *My dad's going to kill me!*

In less than thirty seconds, the symbol was etched on my ankle. I was raised in a *Don't come home if you get a tattoo* environment, so the whole situation felt so forbidden and exciting. I couldn't believe I had gone through with it. As I was admiring my tiny, tiny Chinese symbol, I heard Lil say, "How's it looking?"

I headed to her station and gasped. She was lying belly-down with a GARDEN tattooed across her lower back. "Oh my gosh, that's really big!"

She rolled her eyes and said, "If you're going to be a bear, be a grizzly."

It has been fifteen years since Lil and I got our tattoos. We both ended up getting divorced, then remarried and lost touch in the process. I should have the tattoo removed because it has faded and looks like a smudge of dirt but I must admit, I love when people ask me what it means.

My smudgy tattoo

Every time I tell the story, I get to relive that weekend when we thought we were so old but were just getting our lives started. I think of the beach, the taste of fresh stone crabs and the nervous giggles Lil and I had doing something devilish together. And I smile.

When I was in China, I kept asking people what my tattoo meant. Their responses ranged from "Wealth" to "Gong Bao chicken."

财富 Wealth   锣蟒鸡 Gong Bao Chicken

FIGHT FIGHT

Peter and I have been married for seven years and have jobs/mortgages and four kids so we argue all the time. Normally it goes like this.

Me: Stop yelling. For God's sake, we hear you.

Peter: It doesn't seem like anyone hears me because no one is doing what I asked them to do.

Me: Simmer down. Don't ruin our weekend because someone didn't do exactly what you wanted.

Peter: I talk to the kids because I care about them. I take a lot of time with my kids.

Me: Are you passive-aggressively saying that I don't take time with my kid? Just because you lecture, lecture, lecture doesn't make you a better parent.

Peter gets Jell-O out of the refrigerator and eats it.

Me: Oh my God, will you please stop chomping? That's Jell-O for f*** sake. How can you chomp and slurp on Jell-O?

Peter: You know there are a lot of things that you do that I don't particularly like but I don't bring them up.

Me: Like what?

Peter: I'm not going to say because you're too sensitive.

Me: If you have something to say, say it.

Peter: I'm not that kind of person.

Me: No, you're being a p***y.

Peter: Did you just call me a p***y?

Me: I said you're being one and stop slurping that f*****g Jell-O!

Peter: You know, you can be a real b**** sometimes.

Me: You knew that when you married me.

Peter: You're crazy!

Me: I have conditions!

Peter storms out to take a shower, then returns to the kitchen.

Peter: Babe, you want spicy shrimp for dinner?

Me: Sure.

Unfortunately, in my marriage I sometimes get so enraged I say the worst three words to my spouse: *I hate you.* Then I stomp off to sleep in the guest bedroom. In the morning, when I head down to take a shower, I see Peter, the man I fell in love with, the person I'm doing life with, sleeping so peacefully and I sometimes I think ... I still hate you.

But ... I also love you, so I head to the kitchen and make us avocado toast.

Finito

I believe that all of these experiences will serve a purpose—otherwise, I would be admitted to Lakeview Behavioral Health Hospital.

I was raised in a *don't air your dirty laundry* environment and respect my parents and grandparents for their never-wavering commitment to that philosophy. Obviously, writing a 200+ page book about all my failures demonstrates that the family philosophy didn't work for me.

I feel like a weight is being lifted when I share my failures and fears.[75] Even the Bible tells us to *Share each other's burdens ...* and *encourage one another and build one another up ....*[76]

We all suffer setbacks, disasters, illnesses, failures and humiliations. Sometimes, just saying the words "I made that mistake too" or "I've been there" to a person that is battling guilt and shame is all it takes to free them.

If you've survived, then you have hope, and isn't that all we need? Because, *You* are never a failure—you're just having a little bit of trouble right now.

---

[75] I'm an over sharer.
[76] Galatians 6:2-12, Thessalonians 5:11

The End

REFERENCE GUIDE FOR STORIES

In remembrance of Traci and Caroline.

Calculate Your Perseverance!

Tucked your skirt or dress into your underwear

Locked your keys in the car, with your child still in it

Fired/laid off/ not put on the schedule

Fallen in a public place

Survived a terrible haircut, perm or color

Been dumped

Kicked out of school

Wrecked your car into your other car or your own house

Walked in on someone using the bathroom

During a business meal, realized you have something in your teeth

Been tested for an STD

Worn two different shoes to work

Caught picking your nose

Forgotten someone's name that you had been introduced to before

Clogged a toilet at a friend's house

Fallen off a treadmill/exercise equipment

Waved wildly to someone who wasn't waving to you

Bought something because it was on sale, even though it didn't fit

Struggled with losing those last few pounds

Congratulated someone on their pregnancy when they weren't expecting

Sent nasty email or text to the person you were being nasty about

Suffering from (can be self-diagnosed):

     -OCD – Obsessive Compulsive Disorder

     -Misophonia – certain sounds trigger irritation

     - Dysarthria – trouble with speech, pronunciation

     - Sedatephobia – dislike/discomfort in silence

     - Mom Brain – can't remember anything

Other: _____

Scoring: one point for each item

Less than 5: You're a proper lady and probably would not enjoy hanging out with me.

5-9: You have some issues with holding your s*** together.

Over 10: Join the club! You're a hot mess!

Book Club Discussion Questions

1. The author begins the book sharing that she had been raised in Appalachia. How much impact do you feel geography has on a person's life?

2. If you could erase any of your mistakes, would you? Why or why not?

3. How have you overcome rejection?

4. Do you feel social media adds to your happiness and joy or detracts from it?

5. Do you think children are too protected from failure?

6. Is there truth in the saying "the best things in life are free"?

7. What influence do you feel Hollywood and the media have on women's perceptions of beauty?

8. The author admits to changing herself to maintain a relationship. Have you ever presented yourself differently than you really are?

9. The author doesn't see herself as a failure. Do you agree or disagree with her?

10. After calculating your perseverance tally sheet, do you have any words of wisdom for others that may be going through a difficult time?

Acknowledgements:

This book was the effort of so many talented women. Editing by Greer Tirrill, Ansley Millwood and Sharon Honeycutt. Special thanks for your commitment to the book launch: Kim Hammond, Kristen Ingmire, Andrea Ferenchik and Dr. Myla Bennett. Thank you, Rhiannon Johnson, Allison Futch and Heather Brown for marketing help. Website, www.amylyle.me by Marnie Raines and Debi Smith.

A huge thank you to my tribe for content ideas and/or support for the book including: Sharon Specker, Shannon Krogman, Cheryl Cicha, Jen Pete, Rachel King, Ashley Morgan, Marjorie Presten, Suzanne Yancey, Kristin Upite, Richane Swedenberg, Susie Hale, Sherry Topper, Jami Bresnahan, Meredith Campbell, Michelle Johnson, Cristy Daly, Cori Williams, Krissy Toth, Lisa Ode, Gayle Donaghue, Traci Nicolson, Melissa Green, Susan Vance, Marilyn Mallas, Leslie LaValley, Carie Ann Shaffer, Kathleen Whaley, Jenny Volk, Heather Paton, Dana Kelhofer, Gina Gibb, Kim Paquette. Tracey Henry, Heidi Grew, Peri Sanders and Christina Peterson and my peeps at BB. Dog photos provided by friends: Tabby Carter, Rachael Buffa, Megan Summerville, Mary Delp, Amanda Shires Gina Ryals and Meghan Leigh.

Thank you, to my parents, Beth and Phil Araiza and John Binegar. Thank you, Rodney Henson, my mentor. Thank you, to my one big love for your never-ending support and encouragement, Peter Lyle, and our children, Savannah, Maddy, PJ and Anna.

Amy Lyle is a playwright, actor and screenwriter living in Atlanta with her second husband, Peter, four teenagers and a very large dog.

THE AMY BINEGAR-KIMMES-LYLE BOOK OF FAILURES is her first book.

Visit Amy and share your failures!

WWW.AMYLYLE.ME
AMYLYLE.ME
@AMYLYLE
@AUTHORAMYLYLE

#BOOKOFFAILURES

Cover photos by Andrea Ferenchik.

10% of book proceeds benefit The Place, in Forsyth County, an organization committed to helping people become self-sustaining. www.theplaceofforsyth.org to volunteer or donate.

Made in the USA
Columbia, SC
06 May 2017